MW01700931

A CONCISE INTRODUCTION TO LOGIC

STUDY GUIDE

DANIEL ROTHBART

Department of Philosophy and Religious Studies
George Mason University
Fairfax, Virginia

KENDALL/HUNT PUBLISHING COMPANY
4050 Westmark Drive Dubuque, Iowa 52002

ISBN 0-7872-0958-9

Printed in the United States of America

10 9 8 7 6 5 4 3 2

CONTENTS

Preface

Learning introductory logic requires a thorough understanding of the material and extensive practice from an array of exercises. As such, the primary purpose of this study guide is to highlight the major principles of introductory logic, and to provide answers to many exercises as presented in Patrick J. Hurley's A Concise Introduction to Logic, Fifth Edition, Wadsworth Publishing Company. This study guide should be used as a supplement to, and not a substitute for, Hurley's excellent textbook. The study guide may also accompany Irving M Copi and Carl Cohen, Introduction to Logic, Ninth Edition, Macmillan Publishing Company.

The completion of this work would not be possible without the questions, comments, uncertainties, and successes of my many logic students. But the original inspiration for this project came from William MacFarlane, a masterful logic instructor. Emmett Holman's incisive critical remarks avoided errors in earlier drafts. Finally, I am especially grateful to Nancy Craig for her outstanding and laborious secretarial assistance.

I thank Wadsworth Publishing Company for permission to excerpt portions of Hurley's A Concise Introduction to Logic. Such permission was necessary to complement the content of this textbook. The excerpted material includes the following: all chapter headings and subheadings, definitions to the central logical concepts, and answers to almost 25% of the exercises as presented in "Instructor's Manual for A Concise Introduction to Logic", Fifth Edition, by Patrick Hurley.

The author of this study guide has refused all royalties from purchases at his home institution, George Mason University.

A CONCISE INTRODUCTION TO LOGIC: STUDY GUIDE

Chapter 1: Basic Concepts

Section 1.1: Basic Concepts of Logic

A. What is Logic?

1. Logic = df. the idealized study of reasoning, in the form of arguments, for the purpose of distinguishing successful from unsuccessful cases of reasoning.

2. Successful instance of reasoning:

"New York is north of Washington, D.C. and Washington, D.C. is north of Atlanta. Therefore, New York is north of Atlanta." Why is this successful?

3. Unsuccessful instance of reasoning:

"Miami is north of Washington, D.C. and Washington, D.C. is north of Atlanta. Therefore, Miami is north of Atlanta." Why is this unsuccessful?

B. All instances of reasoning are conveyed as arguments.

1. Argument = df. a finite sequence of statements in which one or more statement is intended to support one other statement.

2. What is the purpose of an argument?

a. The purpose of an argument is to show that the truth of one statement (conclusion) follows from the truth of one or more other statements (reasons).

b. The purpose of an argument is to express a belief transfer: the speaker intends listener to believe the conclusion based on belief of premises.

3. Sometimes an argument fulfills its purpose, but other times it does not.

C. What are the components of an argument?

1. The components of every argument consist of descriptive statements, each of which must be true or false.

2. The components of every argument comprise exactly one conclusion and at least one premise.

a. Conclusion = df. statement being proven, demonstrated, or shown true. The conclusion is not always controversial.

b. Premise = df. statement intended to convince others of conclusion's truth. The premise justifies, demonstrates, explains, or illustrates the conclusion.

Section 1.2: Recognizing Arguments

A. Many passages are not arguments, such as warnings, statements of belief without evidence or reasons, single descriptions, expository passages, and illustrations.

B. An argument arises whenever one statement is intended to provide evidence (reasons) to demonstrate the truth of another.

1. To determine the argument within a passage, first, within an argument search for conclusion.

a. Conclusion can be anywhere within the passage.

b. Conclusion is typically controversial, but not always.

2. Second, search for each premise, as a separate statement intended to support the conclusion.

C. A single conditional statement by itself is not an argument.

1. A conditional statement = df. a compound statement which assumes an 'if . . . , then . . . ' sequence.

a. 'if' is followed by the antecedent.

b. 'then' is followed by the consequent.

2. Example: "If it snows 10 feet tonight in the center of town, then school will close tomorrow." The antecedent is not intended to prove the truth of the consequent; the consequent is not intended to be true.

Section 1.3: Induction versus Deduction

A. Every argument is either deductive or inductive, depending on the intended degree of strength between the argument's premises and conclusion.

B. Deduction

1. A deductive argument = df. an argument in which the conclusion is intended to follow necessarily from the premises. This means that the truth of the conclusion is intended to be guaranteed under the assumption that the premises are true.

2. For example, "All students in this class are philosophy majors, and John is a student in this class. Therefore, John is a philosophy major."

3. Deduction is not always an inference from a general claim about a group of things to a particular claim about a single thing.

C. Induction

1. An inductive argument = df. an argument in which the conclusion is intended to follow probably (not necessarily) from the premises. The purpose of an

inductive argument is to show that the conclusion is probably true assuming that the premises are all true.

2. For example, "95% of the students in this class are philosophy majors, and John is a student in this class. Therefore, John is probably a philosophy major."

3. Induction is not always an inference from a few particular claims about single things to a general claim about a group of things.

Section 1.4: Validity, Truth, Soundness, Strength, Cogency

A. How do we judge the success of a deductive argument?

1. A successful deductive argument must have all true premises.

2. It must have a perfect logical structure between premises and conclusion. What does this mean?

B. A perfect structure of a deductive argument is by definition a valid structure.

1. Validity = df. property of a deductive argument in which the truth of the conclusion follows necessarily from the truth of all the premises.

2. Validity = df. property of a deductive argument in which it is impossible for all the premises to be true and the conclusion to be false in the same context of application.

3. Examples of valid arguments with all true premises

a. "New York is north of Baltimore, and Baltimore is north of Atlanta. Therefore, New York is north of Atlanta."

b. "The number 10 is greater than the number 9, and 9 is greater than

8. So, 10 is greater than 8."

c. "All cities in the USA have more than 1000 inhabitants, and New York is a city in the USA. So, New York has more than 1000 inhabitants."'

4. Examples of valid argument with all false premises.

a. "New York is south of Baltimore, and Baltimore is south of Atlanta. Therefore, New York is south of Atlanta."

b. "The number 10 is less than the number 9, and 9 is less than 8. So, 10 is less than 8."

c. "All cities in the USA have less than 1000 inhabitants, and Paris (France) is a city in the USA. So, Paris (France) has less than 1000 inhabitants."

C. The truth of statements is a very different property from the validity of arguments.

1. The correspondence notion of true defines truth as a correspondence between a statement and some event in the world.

a. Statement S is true = df. S corresponds to (maps onto) a real state of affairs in the world.

2. The actual truth or falsity of the premises does not always determine validity.

3. But we must imagine what would happen to the conclusion under the assumption that the premises are all true.

D. Imperfect structure of a deductive argument is described by the property of invalidity.

1. Invalidity = df. property of a deductive argument in which the truth of the

conclusion does not follow necessarily from the truth of all the premises.

2. Invalidity = df. property of a deductive argument in which it is possible for all the premises to be true and the conclusion false in the same context of application.

3. Examples of invalid arguments with all false premises.

a. "New York is south of Baltimore and Baltimore is south of Atlanta. So, New York is north of Miami."

b. "The number 10 is less than 9 and 9 is less than 8. So, the number 10 is greater than 13."

4. Examples of invalid arguments with all true premises.

a. "New York is north of Baltimore and Baltimore is north of Atlanta. Therefore, New York is north of Miami."

b. "The number 10 is greater than 9 and 9 is greater than 8. So, 10 is less than 13."

E. Successful deductive argument is a sound deductive argument.

1. Sound argument = df. deductive argument with (1) all true premises and with (2) a valid structure.

2. Unsound argument = df. deductive argument without all true premises, or without a valid structure, or without both true premises and a valid structure.

F. Quiz: answer 'true' or 'false' to these claims.

1. Each valid argument must have a true conclusion. (f)

2. Some sound arguments have false conclusions. (f)

3. Each invalid argument must have a false premise.(f)

4. Each invalid argument has either a false premise, or a false conclusion.(f)

5. Each unsound argument has either a false premise or a false conclusion. (f)

6. Some valid arguments are unsound.(t)

G. A successful inductive argument is a cogent inductive argument.

1. A cogent inductive argument = df. an inductive argument in which all the premises are true and the structure is strong. But what does 'strong' mean?

2. Strong inductive argument = df. an inductive argument in which the conclusion probably, but not necessarily, follows from the premises. For a strong inductive argument, if all premises are assumed to be true then it is probable that the conclusion is true.

3. Weak inductive argument = df. an inductive argument in which the conclusion does not follow, even probably, from premises. For weak argument, if all the premises are true then it is not probable that the conclusion is true.

Section 1.5: Argument Forms: Proving Invalidity

A. The counterexample method is a method for proving the invalidity of an argument, but not for proving its validity. This method is grounded on the idea that the central concern in determining the validity or invalidity of the argument is the argument structure.

1. First, isolate the form, or structure, of the argument.

a. The form of the argument is determined by replacing all descriptive words of the subject by some letter, and all the descriptive words of the predicate by another letter.

a. Here is argument #1: "Since some employees are not social climbers and all vice-presidents are employees, we may conclude that some vice-presidents are not social climbers."

b. The form of argument #1 is as follows:

Some E are not S.

All V are E.

Therefore, some V are not S.

2. Second, construct another argument as a substitution instance of this form having all true premises and a false conclusion. Any substitution instance of this form is constructed by replacing the letters E, S, and V by descriptive words.

a. Argument #2 is a substitution instance of this form, as follows:

'Some animals are not mammals.

All dogs are animals.

Therefore, some dogs are not mammals.'

b. Argument #2 is a substitution instance of the form stated above, and has all true premises and a false conclusion. Clearly, argument #2 is invalid.

3. Since argument #2 is an invalid instance of the form, which in turn is the form for argument #1, it follows that argument #1 is also invalid.

B. Thus, invalidity of argument #1 can be proven by constructing another argument, #2, with the same logical form as the #1 but with true premises and a false conclusion.

Section 1.6: Extended Arguments

A. Most editorials, essays, and lengthy letters to newspaper editors assume a complex arrangement of many subarguments. Such an arrangement is described as an extended argument.

B. Each subargument consists of one or more premises supporting one or more conclusions. (Notice that a subargument may have more than one conclusion, but an argument must have exactly one conclusion.)

1. Let every separate statement of the argument be assigned a number, starting with the number 1.

2. Use the arrow to indicate the direction of inference from one or more premises to a single conclusion. So, '(2) --> (1)' means that statement (2) is a premise for the conclusion statement (1).

3. Remember that the conclusion may appear anywhere in the argument.

C. Underlying every extended argument, there are four basic patterns of argumentation.

1. The <u>vertical pattern</u> consists of a series of arguments in which a conclusion of a logically prior argument becomes a premise of a subsequent argument.

a. The particular vertical pattern shown claims that statement (4) supports (3), (3) supports (2), and (2) supports (1).

b. Notice that in this example (3) functions as a conclusion in relation to (4) as well as a premise in relation to (2).

2. The <u>horizontal pattern</u> consists of a single argument in which a single

conclusion is supported by two or more premises, which function independently of each other. Statements (2), (3), and (4) independently support (1). This type of independence means that each of these three statements would function as a premise on behalf of (1) even if the other two were eliminated from the arguments.

3. An argument structure of conjoint premises occurs when two or more statements dependently support a conclusion. This means that, when taken separately, each premise would provide little or no support for the conclusion.

4. An argument structure with multiple conclusions consists of a pattern in which one premise supports two or more conclusions.

a. Since every single argument must have exactly one conclusion, a pattern of multiple conclusions comprises multiple arguments.

b. However, we will treat every multiple conclusion pattern as if it were a single argument by joining the two conclusions with a brace.

Chapter 2: Language: Meaning and Definition

Section 2.1: Cognitive Meaning and Emotive Meaning

A. In everyday conversation our language is used for many different purposes, such as asking questions, telling stories, conveying joy, telling jokes, giving directions, and so on. One important function of our everyday language is to convey the speaker's emotional state, or to evoke an emotive response on the part of the listener.

1. Consider the statement: "The death penalty is a cruel and inhuman form of punishment in which hapless prisoners are dragged from their cells and summarily slaughtered only to satiate the bloodlust of a vengeful public." Many expressions within this statement are intend to evoke an emotionally response: "cruel", "inhuman," "hapless," "dragged", "slaughtered," "bloodlust," and "vengeful".

2. In many cases of deception, the speaker uses emotionally charged expressions to win approval of a controversial conclusion, without appeal to reasoned argument. These expressions are particularly characteristic of mass media advertizing.

B. Frequently, this form of deception occurs when the speaker or writer disguises a controversial value judgment. But from a logical perspective value judgments call for supporting arguments.

1. Although emotive expressions may be unavoidable in certain controversial contexts, such expressions should never be used as substitutes for reasoned defense of a conclusion. This is illustrated by the arguments for the judgment that the death penalty within the criminal justice system is morally permissible (or impermissible).

2. Within logic we are expected to identify the value judgment of the speaker

and to evaluate whether sufficiently strong reasons are provided on behalf of the value judgment.

Section 2.2: The Intension and Extension of Terms

A. The analysis and evaluation of an argument requires a clear understanding of the words of the argument.

1. Terms comprise an important class of words.

2. A term = df. any word or arrangement of words that may serve as the grammatical subject of a statement. Terms consist of proper names, common names, and descriptive phrases.

3. Words that are not terms include verbs, nonsubstantive adjectives, adverbs, prepositions, and conjunctions.

B. We must distinguish between the <u>use</u> of a word and the <u>mention</u> of a word.

1. In the statement "The word 'black' has five letters," the word "black" is being mentioned. The subject is the quoted word rather than the color.

2. In the statement "The color of my shoes is black", the word "black" is used to convey a certain color, attributable to my shoes. Of course, the statement may be false, but the word "black" is being used.

C. Many philosophers have distinguished between the intensional meaning (connotation) of a term and the extensional meaning (denotation) of a term.

1. The extensional meaning of a term consists of the class of entities that the term denotes.

a. To understand extensional meaning, imagine that a term refers to a certain class of entities, regardless of the number of members of the class. The denotation of the term consists of this class of entities.

b. The extensional meaning of a term may change depending on which members, if any, comprise the term's denotation. For example, the term "current U. S. President by the name of Ronald Reagan" had a particular extension in the past, but now has no extension (empty extension).

2. The intensional meaning of a term consists of the attributes that, collectively, determine membership into the denotation of a term.

a. For example, the intensional meaning of "cats" comprises certain attributes, which determine membership into the term's denotation.

b. According to some philosophers, the intensional meaning of a term is the term's conventional connotation, which comprises the attributes that the term commonly, but not necessarily, connotes. Usually, the term's conventional connotation does not change over time.

D. A series of terms has an increasing extension when the series refers to an increasing number of members.

1. A series of terms displaying increasing extension are as follows: "tiger", "feline", "mammal", "animal".

2. Notice that as the extension increases in this scale of terms, the number of attributes determining membership in this scale decreases. Requirements for membership into the class of mammals is, as it were, more lax in relation to requirements for

membership into the class of animals.

3. As a general rule, increasing extension of a series of terms is usually associated with decreasing number of attributes comprising intensional meaning. This rule is not fulfilled in cases where the extension is empty.

Section 2.3: Definitions and Their Purposes

A. Every definition assigns a meaning to some word or group of words.

1. A definiendum = df. the word or group of words that is presumably being defined.

2. A definiends = df. the word or group of words that presumably provides meaning to the definiendum.

B. Different types of definitions can be distinguished by their purposes.

1. Stipulative definitions

a. Assume a context in which some entity, process, or idea is newly discovered or conceived.

b. For every stipulative definition, meaning is assigned to a word or group of words through a deliberate act of designation (or baptizism) by an individual or group of individuals to a newly discovered, or conceived, entity.

c. A stipulative definition assigns a meaning to a word for the first time.

2. Lexical definitions

a. Assume that a word or group of words is already defined by a community of speakers.

b. For every lexical definition, meaning is assigned to a word or group of words (the definiendum) based on a report of the way in which the definiendum is already used in the language.

c. Most dictionary definitions are lexical definitions, because each dictionary definition conveys how a community of speakers uses a definiendum.

d. Ideally, lexical definitions should minimize vagueness and ambiguity.

(1) Vagueness

(a) A word is vague within a particular context of application when, by definition, it is impossible to determine whether or not the word is attributable to some entity, process, or idea within that context. For such borderline cases, the truth or falsity of the statement containing a vague word may be undetermined.

(b) Although most words display some degree of vagueness within certain contexts, a well-reasoned argument should use words that minimize vagueness.

(2) Ambiguity

(a) A word is ambiguous within a particular context of application when, by definition, it is possible to provide two or more clearly distinct meanings of the word within a given context.

(b) While a vague word does not permit a single precise meaning within a particular context, an ambiguous word provides two or more meanings within a context.

(c) The word "right" can be used to convey the correct answer, the morally prudent action, or the opposite to left.

(d) Within argumentation, ambiguous words should be minimized, or when they occur a single meaning should be obvious from the context.

3. Precising Definitions

a. Assume a context in which a word or group of words is used in a relatively vague way.

b. A precising definition provides meaning to a definiendum in such a way that the vagueness of the word or group of words is reduced, in comparison to the meaning from a previous definition. The meaning provided by a precising definition reduces the degree of vagueness of the word or group of words.

c. Typically, precising definitions are common to technical contexts, such as science, medicine, or law for the purpose of reducing vagueness to the degree that is appropriate within a particular context.

4. Theoretical Definitions

a. For every theoretical definition the meaning attributable to the definiendum consists of a conceptual representation, or mental image, of an entity or process.

b. For example, a theoretical definition of "heat" provides a meaning with respect to the conceptual picture of energy associated with the random motion of molecules of a substance.

5. Persuasive Definitions

a. Assume a context in which the speaker or writer misuses certain words for the purpose of trying to influence the attitudes of an audience.

b. A persuasive definition arises when the meaning of a word or group of words which is familiar to the community of speakers is changed to an emotionally charged or value-laden meaning. Masquerading as an honest assignment of meaning, the persuasive definition is used as an instrument of persuasion.

Section 2.4: Definitional Techniques

A. Every extensional definition assigns meaning by indicating, in some way, the class of entities that the definiendum denotes. The three ways in which this assignment of meaning can be accomplished correspond to three types of extensional definitions.

1. A demonstrative (ostensive) definition provides an extensional definition by the act of pointing to the class of entities that the definiendum denotes. This definition confers meaning by pointing to the extension of the definiendum. For example, "Chair" means this and this and this--as you point to a number of chairs.

2. An enumerative definition provides an extensional definition by the act of naming the members of the class of entities that the definiendum denotes. But frequently, an enumerative definition provides a partial list of members of the class, because the class may be excessively large. For example, "actor" means a person such as Nick Nolte, Al Pacino, or Richard Gere.

3. A definition by subclass provides an extensional definition by the act of naming subclasses of the extension of the definiendum. Again, such a definition may be

partial, when the subclasses named do not exhaust all member of the class. For example, "tree" means an oak, pine, elm, spruce, maple, and the like.

B. An intensional definition obviously must assign an intensional meaning to the definiendum. As we learned above, an intensional meaning of a term consists of the attributes that, collectively, determine membership into the denotation of the definiendum. There are four strategies for assigning intensional meaning, corresponding to four types of intensional definitions.

1. A <u>synonymous definition</u> provides the intensional meaning of a definiendum in the form of a single word. For example, "physician" means doctor.

2. An <u>etymological definition</u> provides the intensional meaning by disclosing the term's ancestry from past uses of the definiendum in our own, or other, languages. Typically, an etymological definition is provided by the Latin origins of the term.

3. An <u>operational definition</u> provides intensional meaning by specifying the (operational) conditions under which the definiendum is attributable to some entity, process, or event. If these operational conditions are fulfilled, then the definiendum is correctly applicable to an entity, process, or event. For example, if an electroencephalograph show oscillations when attached to the subject's head, then the subject as "brain activity".

4. A <u>definition by genus and difference</u> provides intensional meaning by identifying a genus term and one or more difference words.

a. In logic the genus is the attribute which identifies a relatively larger class of entities that subsumes the denotation of the definiendum. For example, the genus for "daughter" is offspring, because the class of offspring subsumes the class of daughters.

b. In logic the difference is the (differentiating) attribute which identifies one subclass of the genus, in contrast to one or more other subclasses. For example, the difference for "daughter" is female, because the attribute of being female differentiates one subclass of offspring from the other subclass of offspring.

Section 2.5: Criteria for Lexical Definitions

A. Consider some rules for constructing lexical definitions and for evaluating lexical definitions of others.

1. Rule 1: A lexical definition should conform to the standards of proper grammar.

2. Rule 2: A lexical definition should convey the essential meaning of the word being defined.

3. Rule 3: A lexical definition should be neither too broad by including too many entities within the denotative meaning, nor too narrow by excluding entities that should comprise part of the denotative meaning.

4. Rule 4: a lexical definition should not be circular. Circularity occurs when the definiends itself is defined by the definiendum.

5. Rule 5: A lexical definition should not be negative, where an affirmative definition is appropriate. A proper definition should not convey what the definiendum does not mean, when the definition can be affirmative.

6. Rule 6: A lexical definition should not be expressed in figurative, obscure, vague, or ambiguous language.

7. Rule 7: a lexical definition should avoid, or at least minimize, affective terminology, which is terminology that exploits the emotional sentiments of the reader or listener.

8. Rule 8: A lexical definition should indicate the context to which the definiends pertains.

Chapter 3: Informal Fallacies

Section 3.1: Fallacies in General and Section 3.2: Fallacies of Relevance

A. There are two types of fallacies.

1. Formal Fallacy = df. a type of defect in the argument structure.

a. The argument appears to be valid, but is not.

b. For example, 'All A are B. All C are B. Therefore, All A are C.'

2. Informal Fallacy = df. a type of defect in the content of the argument, but not in the structure.

a. Although every informal fallacy is defined as a defect in the content of the argument, most examples of informal fallacies also exhibit defects in structure as well. This is because more instances of an informal fallacy are invalid arguments.

b. So, we should not assume that every argument that commits an informal fallacy is formally correct (valid). Similarly, we should not assume that every argument that commits a formal fallacy avoids all the informal fallacies.

B. All fallacies in Section 3.2 are informal fallacies of relevance, which means that the premises are logically irrelevant for the purpose of demonstrating the truth of the conclusion. (All instances of fallacies of relevance are also invalid arguments.)

1. Appeal to force occurs when the arguer poses a conclusion to another person, and threatens harm in order to coerce the listener to accept the conclusion. The threat may be physical or emotional; it may be implicit or explicit.

2. Appeal to Pity occurs when the arguer poses a conclusion and evokes pity from the listener in an effort to win acceptance of the conclusion.

3. Appeal to the People has two forms.

a. The direct form arises when the arguer excites emotions and enthusiasms of the crowd in order to win acceptance of the conclusion, as illustrated by episodes of political flag waving. Typically, the direct form of appeal to the people is committed in certain emotionally charged words.

b. The indirect approach occurs when arguer appeals to one or more individuals separately, focusing on some relationship to the crowd.

(1)Bandwagon argument

(2)Appeal to vanity

(3)Appeal to snobbery

4. Argument against the person has 3 forms. For each form assume that person #1 advances an argument to person #2.

a. Ad hominem abusive occurs when person #2 responds by verbally abusing the character of #1. This abuse is fallacious within the context of an argument, even if the abusive characteristics are true.

b. Ad hominem circumstantial occurs when #2 attempts to discredit the argument by referring to certain circumstances that influence person #1.

(1)This response by #2 suggests that #1 is biased, or controlled by other people.

(2)Such an attack is irrelevant to demonstrating the truth or falsity of the conclusion.

a. Tu quoque (You, too) "2 wrongs make a right" occurs when #2 replies to an accusation by shifting the burden of guilt back to #1.

5. Accident occurs when a general rule is cited in the premises and wrongly applied to a specific (atypical) case in the conclusion. This is a misapplication of an otherwise correct rule.

6. Straw Man again assumes that person #1 advances a position to #2. Straw man occurs when #2 responds by distorting what #1 said, and then attacking the distorted version of #1's argument.

7. Missing the point occurs when the premises of an argument support one particular conclusion, but then a different conclusion, often vaguely related to the correct conclusion, is drawn.

8. Red herring again assumes that person #1 advances a position to #2. Red herring occurs when the arguer changes the subject to a different issue, and draws a conclusion about a different issue.

Section 3.3: Fallacies of Weak Induction

The error underlying all the fallacies in this section is the inadequate degree of support that the premises confer on the conclusion. Fallacies of weak induction assume that the premises are not nearly strong enough to support the conclusion, even though the premises may include some evidence.

A. The appeal to unqualified authority

1. Assume that an arguer cites the authority or testimony of another person in support of some conclusion.

2. The fallacy is committed when the cited authority is not trustworthy, because a lack of relevant expertise, biased character, ulterior motive, or inability to perceive or recall.

3. The judgment that a person is untrustworthy as an authority must be based on clear, reasonably obvious factors.

B. Appeal to Ignorance

1. Assume that nothing has been proven one way or another about a particular subject.

2. The fallacy is committed when the arguer then renders a definite assertion about that subject.

3. Typically, the fallacy is committed when someone argues that because no evidence has been found against the existence of some event, the event must be real.

4. Exceptions.

b. If qualified researchers fail to discover evidence on behalf of some alleged event, then this lack of evidence constitutes as least partial evidence against the event ever occurring.

c. In the US criminal judicial system, the failure of the prosecution to prove the guilt of the defendant beyond reasonable doubt, the defendant may be found to be not guilty.

C. Hasty Generalization

1. The fallacy of hasty generalization is committed when the arguer appeals to a select and atypical sample of a group to draw a generalization in the conclusion about all

members of a group.

2. The sample must be too small and atypical to be representative of the diversity of the group.

D. False Cause

1. The fallacy of false cause is committed when the success of the argument depends on some imagined causal connection that does not actually exist.

2. The identification of this fallacy assumes that the reader knows that the alleged causal connection is spurious.

3. Sub-types of false cause fallacies.

a. Post hoc ergo propter hoc means "after this, therefore on account of this". This fallacy is committed when causation is attributed to an event merely because that event preceded the alleged effect in time.

b. Non causa pro causa means "not the cause for the cause". This is committed when the arguer mistakenly attributes a causal relation between the events, where the mistake is other than mere temporal succession.

c. Oversimplified cause is committed when the arguer incorrectly selects only one cause as being responsible for an effect, where a multitude of causes are actually responsible.

E. Slippery Slope

1. This fallacy is committed when an arguer assumes a belief in a chain reaction of events, where little or no evidence exists on behalf of this belief.

2. Usually, this fallacy is committed when the arguer alleges that the chain

reaction leads to some dire, or dangerous event at the end of the slippery slope.

F. Weak Analogy

1. Assume that some argument conveys an analogy, or similarity, between two subjects, such as things or situations. In an argument from analogy the speaker or writer, first, identifies in the premises certain known similarities between the two subjects in question, and, second, proposes in the conclusion that a particular property of one subject can be attributed to the other subject of the analogy.

2. The fallacy of weak analogy is committed when the similarity relations conveyed by the premises are not strong enough to support the conclusion that a property of one subject is attributable to the other subject.

Section 3.4: Fallacies of Presumption, Ambiguity, and Grammatical Analogy

A. Fallacies of presumption are fallacies that assume in the premises what is presumably being proven in the conclusion. The four fallacies of presumption are begging the question, complex question, false dichotomy, and suppressed evidence.

1. Begging the question occurs when an arguer uses some form of phraseology that tends to conceal the questionable (controversial) character of a premise.

a. This concealment tends to disguise the fact that one premise may be false.

b. Typically, this concealment is accomplished by phrasing the argument in such a way that the premise and conclusion say the same thing, but in slightly different ways.

2. Complex Question

a. Assume that a question is asked in such a way that any answer presumes an answer to another (suppressed) question.

b. The fallacy of complex question is committed when an answer to the explicit question is applied to answer the suppressed question.

c. This fallacy is used typically for the purpose of trapping the respondent into acknowledging an unintended claim.

3. False dichotomy

a. The fallacy of false dichotomy is committed when one premise of an argument presents two mutually exclusive alternatives, although in fact the subject matter of the argument calls for more than the two alternatives presented.

b. Typically, false dichotomy arises when alternatives to some problem are falsely presented in an "either . . . or . . . " manner.

4. Suppressed evidence

a. For any cogent inductive argument, the premises should not ignore some important piece of evidence that outweighs the evidence presented in the premises.

b. The fallacy of suppressed evidence arises when an inductive argument does indeed ignore such evidence. When the fallacy is committed, the speaker or writer attempts to ignore evidence that would support an alternative conclusion.

B. Fallacies of ambiguity arise from the occurrence of some form of ambiguity in the premise or the conclusion. Again, a term is ambiguous if it is susceptible to different meanings in a given context. Two of these fallacies are equivocation and amphibole.

1. The fallacy of <u>equivocation</u> occurs when the conclusion of an argument depends on the fact that one or more words are used, either explicitly or implicitly, in two different senses in the argument.

2. The fallacy of <u>amphibole</u>

a. Assume that some argument includes a statement that is ambiguous due to a defect in the structure of the statement.

b. The fallacy of amphibole occurs when the arguer misinterprets a statement because of this structural ambiguity, and then draws a conclusion based on this misinterpretation.

c. Amphibole arises from a defect in the structure of the statement, whereas equivocation arises from an ambiguity in the meaning of one or more words.

C. Fallacies of grammatical analogy include <u>composition</u> and <u>division</u>.

1. The fallacy of <u>composition</u> is committed when the conclusion of an argument depends on the erroneous transfer of an attribute from parts of an entity to the whole entity.

a. Again, composition is committed when the arguer claims that the whole entity has a property on the grounds that its parts have that property, in spite of the fact that this transfer of the property is erroneous.

b. Not every transfer of a property from parts of an entity to the whole entity is associated with composition. Notice that the fallacy arises when this transfer is unwarranted.

2. The fallacy of <u>division</u> is committed when the arguer claims that the

property attributable to the whole entity is attributable, erroneously, to parts of the entity.

a. Division assumes the transfer of a property from the whole to its parts, whereas composition assumes the transfer of a property from parts of an entity to the whole entity.

b. In order for division to be committed, the transfer from the whole entity to its parts must be unwarranted.

Section 3.5: Detecting Fallacies in Ordinary Language

Identification of a fallacy within an argument can become a rather challenging endeavor. In many cases the fallacious character of the argument centers on a subtle error, which may be distinguished within an otherwise well-reasoned argument. In other cases more than one fallacy is committed in a single argument. Another problem arises when the arguments in ordinary language are not presented in a complete form. A premise or a conclusion may be omitted, necessitating the reader or listener to speculate about the content of the unexpressed statement.

Chapter 4: Categorical Propositions

Section 4.1: The Components of Categorical Propositions

A. This chapter addresses the logic underlying categorical propositions. What is a categorical proposition?

1. For all practical purposes in this text, every proposition is a statement that must be either true or false.

2. Every categorical proposition is a statement that must convey some relationship between two categories or classes, depicted by a subject term and a predicate term.

3. A categorical proposition = df. a proposition that asserts that either all or part of the class denoted by the subject term is included in, or excluded from, the class denoted by the predicate terms.

4. From this definition there are four standard forms in term of which a categorical proposition can be formulated.

a. "All S are P" implies that the entire subject class S is included in the predicate class P.

b. "No S are P" implies that the entire subject class S is excluded from the predicate class P.

c. "Some S are P" implies that part of S is included within P.

d. "Some S are not P" implies that part of S is excluded from P.

C. Elements of every categorical statement.

1. Quantifier terms: all, no, some

a. 'All' refers to each and every member of some subject class.

b. 'No' refers also to each and every member of some subject class which is <u>not</u> being ascribed a certain property.

c. 'Some' is much more ambiguous, referring to <u>at least</u> one member of a class. Notice that 'some' does not necessarily rule out a reference to all members of the subject class.

2. Subject term: class term

3. Predicate term: class term

4. Copula: are, are not

D. The four standard forms of categorical propositions are:

1. All S are P.

2. No S are P.

3. Some S are P.

4. Some S are not P.

Section 4.2: Quality, Quantity, and Distribution

A. Quality of a categorical proposition = df. property of a categorical proposition which is either an affirmative attribution of a predicate to a subject, or a negative attribution of a predicate to a subject.

1. An affirmative attribution means that the subject class <u>S</u> is included within the scope of the predicate class <u>P</u>.

a. All S are P.

b. Some S are P.

2. A negative attribution means that the subject class S is excluded from the scope of the predicate class P.

a. No S are P.

b. Some S are not P.

B. Quantity of a categorical statement = df. property of a categorical proposition which is either universal attribution of a subject class or a particular attribution of a subject class.

1. Universal attribution means that every member of the subject class is, or is not, a member of the predicate class.

a. All S are P.

b. No S are P.

2. Particular attribution means that one or more member of the subject class is, or is not, a member of the predicate class.

a. Some S are P.

b. Some S are not P.

C. Summary

Statement	Name	Quantity	Quality
1. All S are P.	A	Universal	Affirmative
2. No S are P.	E	Universal	Negative
3. Some S are P.	I	Particular	Affirmative
4. Some S are not P	O	Particular	Negative

Section 4.3: The Modern Square of Opposition

A. The problem of existence.

1. For some true categorical propositions the subject term refers to real entities. The statement 'All sodas are carbonated' is a true A-proposition with a subject class that is real.

2. But for other true categorical propositions the subject term does not refer to real entities. 'All Martians are creatures that come from Mars' is a true A-proposition with a subject class that does not exist.

3. We need an interpretation of categorical propositions which does not always require existence of the subject class.

B. We can use a Boolean interpretation of A-propositions and E-propositions in such a way that does not require existence of the subject classes from such propositions.

1. A: "All S are P" does not require existence of S class.

a. "No member of S class is outside of P class."

b. For example, "All Martians are creatures that come from Mars" means "No Martian is outside of the class of things from Mars".

c. The Boolean interpretation of the A-proposition implies that if the subject class of an A-proposition is empty, as in the case of the class of Martians, then the proposition must be true.

d. Another way to understand the Boolean interpretation of an A-proposition is to think of it as a conditional statement: "If an individual is an S, then it is also P".

2. E: "No S are P" does not require existence of S class.

a. "No member of S class is inside of P class."

b. For example, "No unicorn has two horns" means "No unicorn is included within the category of two-horned creatures."

c. The Boolean interpretation of the E-proposition implies that if the subject class of an E-proposition is empty, as in the case of the class of unicorns, then the proposition must be true.

d. "If an individual is an S, then it is not a P."

C. However, the Boolean interpretation does require existence of the subject classes for I-propositions and O-propositions.

1. I: "Some S are P" does require existence of some members of S.

a. "At least one S exists, and that S is also a P."

b. This particular statement assumes existence of the subject class.

2. O: "Some S are not P" does require existence of some members of S.

a. "At least one S exists, and that S is not a P."

b. This particular statement assumes existence.

D. What are the logical relationships between A, E, I, O propositions?

1. The Modern Square conveys a contradictory relation between A-proposition and O-proposition, as well as the contradictory relation between E-proposition and I-proposition. No other logical relation is established between any other pair of categorical propositions.

2. Contradictory relationship

a. Categorical propositions P and Q are contradictories of each other if and only if they always have opposite truth values.

b. P = "All students in this class are enrolled in logic."

Q = "Some students in this class are not enrolled in logic."

3. For every A-proposition there is some O-proposition which is the contradictory of A. For every I-proposition there is some E-proposition which is the contradictory of I. All other combination of statements yields indeterminate truth values.

E. From the modern square of opposition, validity can be determined.

1. Assume that a premise has an A-form and that the conclusion is Not-O. This argument must be valid.

2. Assume that a premise has an E-form and that the conclusion is I. The argument must be invalid.

3. Assume that a premise is I and conclusion is Not-O. The argument must be invalid.

Section 4.4: Conversion, Obversion, Contraposition

There are three ways to change a categorical proposition, based on the operations of conversion, obversion, and contraposition.

A. Conversion

1. The converse of a categorical proposition is formed by switching the subject term with the predicate term, and making no other change.

2. Application

a. A: "All S are P" becomes "All P are S".

b. E: "No S are P" becomes "No P are S".

c. I: "Some S are P" becomes "Some P are S".

d. O: "Some S are not P" becomes "Some P are not S".

3. What is the logical relationship between a categorical proposition and its converse?

a. A is not logically equivalent to its converse.

b. E is equivalent to its converse. no

c. I is equivalent to its converse. some

d. O is not equivalent to its converse.

4. Based on the logical relationships between a categorical proposition and its converse, validity of an argument is established when the statement is equivalent to its converse.

B. Obversion

1. The obverse of a proposition is formed by, first, changing the quality of the proposition and, second, replacing the predicate term with its term complement. (The term complement of a class refers to all objects outside of the class.)

2. Application

a. A: "All S are P" becomes "No S are non-P".

b. E: "No S are P" becomes "All S are non-P".

c. I: "Some S are P" becomes "Some S are not non-P".

d. O: "Some S are not P" becomes "Some S are non-P".

3. Logical relationship between a categorical statement and its obverse.

a. A is equivalent to its obverse.

b. E is equivalent to its obverse

c. I is equivalent to its obverse

d. O is equivalent to its obverse.

4. Whenever an argument is formed by a categorical statement and its obverse, the argument is valid.

C. Contraposition

1. The contraposition of a statement is formed by, first, replacing the subject and predicate by their respective term complements, and second, by switching the placement of the new subject with the placement of the new predicate.

2. Application.

a. A: "All S are P" becomes "All non-P are non-S".

b. E: "No S are P" becomes "No non-P are non-S".

c. I: 'Some S are P' becomes 'Some non-P are non-S'.

d. O: "Some S are not P" becomes "Some non-P are not non-S".

3. Logical relationship between a categorical statement and its contrapositive.

all a. A is logically equivalent to it contrapositive.

b. E is not equivalent to its contrapositive.

c. I is not equivalent to its contrapositive.

Some are not d. O is equivalent to its contrapositive.

4. Based on the logical relationships between a categorical statement and its

contrapositive, the validity of an argument arises when the statement is equivalent to its contrapositive.

Section 4.5: The Traditional Square of Opposition

All
No

A. Again, the Boolean interpretation does not require existence for subject-class of A and E propositions. But another interpretation, called the Traditional Square of Opposition, is more informative than the Boolean interpretation. The Traditional Square is applicable to any categorical proposition as long as the subject class of the proposition is not empty.

B. The Traditional Square is defined by four logical relationships between certain pairs of categorical propositions.

1. Contradictory relationship

a. As we saw above, categorical propositions P and Q are contradictories of each other if and only if they always have opposite truth values.

b. P = "All students in class are enrolled in logic."

Q = "Some students in this class are not enrolled in logic."

c. For every A there is some O which is the contradictory of A. For every I there is some E which is the contradictory of I.

2. Contrary Relationship

a. Categorical propositions P and Q are contraries of each other if and only if they can never both be true together. (At least one must be false.)

b. P = "All students in this class are enrolled in logic."

Q = "No student in this class is enrolled in logic."

c. For every A there is some E which is the contrary of A.

3. Subcontrary relationship

a. Categorical propositions P and Q are subcontraries of each other if and only if they can never both be false together. (At least one must be true.)

b. P = "Some students in this class are enrolled in logic."

Q = "Some students in this class are not enrolled in logic."

c. For every I there is some O which is the subcontrary of I.

4. Subalternation relationship

a. Statements P and Q are subalternations of each other if and only if, first, the inference from P to Q is truth preserving (creating a valid argument), and second, the inference from Q to P is falsity preserving.

b. P = "All students in this class are enrolled in logic."

Q = "Some students in this class are enrolled in logic."

c. For every A there is some I which is the subalternation of A, assuming that both statements have the same subject and predicate.

d. For every E there is some O which is the subalternation of E, assuming that both statements have the same subject and predicate.

C. Based on these four definitions, the traditional square of opposition shows necessary relationships between categorical statements. When a necessary relationship is established between categorical statements, a valid argument is formed.

1. If an A is true, must the I be true? Yes

2. If an E is false, must the O be true? No

4.6: Translating Ordinary Language Statements into Categorical Form

A. Reasoned argumentation become much more problematic with statement that are ambiguous or vague. In some cases one way to minimize these problems is to translate ordinary language statements into categorical propositions in standard forms. Following such translation, we can then apply the logical concepts and operations appropriate for categorical propositions.

B. Rules for translation into categorical form.

1. Rule: if a term consists of only an adjective, then a plural noun or pronoun should be introduced to make the term genuinely denotative. This rule is needed to insure that every subject term and predicate term of a categorical proposition clearly denotes the class of entities indicated by the term.

2. Rule: the verb form must be translated in such a way that incorporates is (are) or is not (are not). This rule rests on the requirement that the only copulas that are allowed in standard form categorical propositions are "is", "are", "is not", "are not".

3. Rule: If a propositions is singular, which means that it makes an assertion about a specific person, place, thing, or time, then the proposition must incorporate a universal statement. For example, "George went home" is translated as "All persons identical to George are persons who went home". In this example, the name "George" is replaced in the statement by "All persons identical to George are person who . . . ", which generates a universal statement.

4. Rule: A statement containing a spatial adverb, such as "where," "wherever," "anywhere," everywhere," or nowhere" may be translated in terms of "places";

a statement containing a temporal adverb, such as "when," "whenever," "anytime," "always," or "never," may be translated in terms of "times"; a statement containing pronouns such as "who," "whoever," "anyone," "what," "whatever," or "anything" may be translated in terms of "person" or "things," respectively.

5. Rule: If a statement assumes a quantifier that is not expressed, then the appropriate quantifier must be made explicit in a universal form or a particular form. For example, "A tiger is a mammal" is translated as "All tigers are mammals".

6. Rule: If a statement assumes a quantity that is not expressed in the standard categorical form, then a translation is appropriate to insure that the quantity is expressed appropriately, so that the statement begins with "All", "No", or "Some". For example, "Not a single dog is a cat" is translated as "No dogs are cats". Notice that the statement form "All S are not P" is not in standard categorical form, because it permits one of two standard forms: "No S are P" or "Some S are not P".

7. Rule: Various conditional statements can be translated into categorical propositions. When the antecedent and consequent of a conditional statement include refer to the same subject by their respective subject terms, the conditional statement can be replaced by a universal statement. When the word "if" occurs in the middle of a conditional statement, the statement can be restructured so that it occurs in the beginning. Also, the word "unless" can be translated as "if not", which of course necessitates a conditional statement.

8. Rule: If a categorical statement contains the words "only", "none but", "none except", or "no . . . except", then the statement can be translated into a universal

form with the terms reversed. The statement "Only friends of John attended the party" is translated as "All persons who attended the party are friends of John".

9. Rule: If a categorical statement begins with the words "The only", then that statement can be translated as "All", which is placed in the beginning of a universal statement.

10. Rule: If a statement has the form "all except S are P", then the statement can be translated as the following pair of conjoined categorical statements: "No S are P and all non-S are P".

Chapter 5: Categorical Syllogisms

Section 5.1: Standard Form, Mood, and Figure

A. What is a categorical syllogism?

1. Roughly speaking, a categorical syllogism is a deductive argument with two premises and one conclusion. There are exactly three different terms in the argument, each appearing twice in distinct propositions.

2. The three terms are named, depending on their positions in the argument.

a. The major term = df. the term conveying the predicate of the conclusion.

b. The minor term = df. the term conveying the subject of the conclusion.

c. The middle term = df. the term occurring once in each premise, but not in the conclusion.

3. Premises.

a. Major premise = df. premise containing the major term.

b. Minor premise = df. premise containing the minor term.

B. What are the requirements for the standard form of a categorical syllogism?

1. All three statements must be standard-form categorical propositions, based on the requirements for A, E, I, and O categorical propositions.

2. The two occurrences of each term are identical. Each term is used in the same sense throughout the argument.

3. The major premise is listed first, the minor premise second, and the

conclusion last.

C. A categorical syllogism = df. a deductive argument which consists of three categorical propositions, and this argument is capable of being translated into standard form. Each simple statement must be translatable into standard form.

D. To determine validity or invalidity of a categorical syllogism, we must inspect the mood and the figure of the syllogism.

1. The mood of a categorical syllogism is determined by the kind of propositions that comprise the syllogism.

a. First, put the syllogism into standard form, with the appropriate letter name for each proposition.

b. Second, determine the mood by conveying the order of these letters, with major premise preceding minor premise, which precedes conclusion.

2. The figure of a syllogism is determined by the placement of the middle term, based on four different possibilities.

3. Then check the mood and figure with the list of unconditionally valid syllogistic forms applicable for a Boolean interpretation of categorical propositions, as presented in Section 5.1.

4. Alternatively, check the mood and figure with the list of conditionally valid syllogistic forms applicable for an Aristotelian interpretation of categorical propositions. This list includes all the unconditionally valid syllogistic forms for the Boolean interpretation.

Section 5.2: Venn Diagrams

A. Venn diagrams provide a relatively easy method for testing the validity of a categorical syllogism.

B. The application of Venn diagrams to a syllogism requires three overlapping circles.

1. Draw three overlapping circles so that seven areas are clearly distinguishable within the diagram.

2. Provide a label for each circle, with each label corresponding to a term.

3. Shade in those particular areas that are necessary to convey the information of each premise, based on the categorical-form of the premise.

a. The diagram for each premise is conveyed by two circles, since each circle represents one of the terms of the premise.

b. Universal propositions should be diagrammed before particular ones.

4. Inspect the diagram to see whether it contains the information within the conclusion.

a. No marks are made for the conclusion.

b. If the information of the conclusion is contained within the diagram, then the argument if valid; otherwise, it is invalid.

Section 5.3: Rules and Fallacies

A. There are five rules that must not be violated in order for the syllogism to be valid. If any rule is violated, then a formal fallacy is committed, and thus the syllogism is invalid.

B. Each rule rests on the notion of the distribution of a term within a proposition.

Distribution is an attribute of the terms (subject and predicate) within a proposition. A term is distributed if the proposition makes an assertion about every member of the class denoted by the term; otherwise, the term is undistributed.

1. For a proposition of the form "All S are P", only the S-term is distributed.

2. For a proposition of the form "No S are P", the S-term and P-term are distributed.

3. For a proposition of the form "Some S and P", neither term is distributed.

4. For a proposition of the form "Some S and not P", only the P-term is distributed.

C. Rules and corresponding fallacies

1. Rule 1: The middle term must be distributed at least once.

a. If this rule is violated, then the fallacy of undistributed middle is committed.

b. Consider an argument in which the fallacy is committed:

"All sharks are fish.

All salmon are fish.

Therefore, all salmon are sharks."

2. Rule 2: If a term is distributed in the conclusion, then it must be distributed in a premise.

a. If this rule is violated, then the fallacy of illicit major or the fallacy of illicit minor is committed.

b. Consider an argument in which the fallacy of illicit major is committed:

"All horses are animals.

Some dogs are not horses.

Therefore, some dogs are not animals."

c. The fallacy of illicit minor is committed in the following:

"All tigers are mammals.

All mammals are animals.

Therefore, all animals are tigers."

3. Rule 3: Two negative premises are not allowed. Recall that a negative categorical proposition has either an E-form or an O-form.

a. The fallacy that corresponds to this rule is called the fallacy of exclusive premises.

b. An instance of this fallacy is the following:

"No fish are mammals.

Some dogs are not fish.

Therefore, some dogs are not mammals."

4. Rule 4: A negative premise requires a negative conclusion, and a negative conclusion requires a negative premise.

a. If this rule is violated, the syllogism illustrates the fallacy of drawing an affirmative conclusion from a negative premise, or drawing a negative conclusion from an affirmative premises.

b. Consider an example of drawing an affirmative conclusion from a negative premise.

"All crows are birds.

Some wolves are not crows.

Therefore, some wolves are birds."

c. Consider an example of drawing a negative conclusion from affirmative premises.

"All triangles are three-angled polygons.

All three-angled polygons are three-sided polygons.

Therefore, three-signed polygons are not triangles."

5. Rule 5: If both premises are universal, then the conclusion cannot be particular.

a. Violation of this rule generates an instance of the existential fallacy.

b. Consider an example of this fallacy:

"All mammals are animals.

All unicorns are mammals.

Therefore, some unicorns are animals."

c. Of course, such an argument would be valid from the standpoint of Aristotelian logic but not within Boolean logic.

Section 5.4: Reducing the Number of Terms

A. Many categorical syllogisms that occur in ordinary spoken or written language are not expressed precisely in the standard-form.

1. The goal is to produce an argument consisting of three standard-form categorical propositions that contain exactly three different terms, each term occurring twice in distinct propositions. But many arguments contain more than the three terms that are required for the standard form.

2. Certain techniques enable one to reduce the number of terms to three.

B. Consider an argument with more than three terms, including two terms that are complements of each other, such as A and non-A. In such a case, one of these terms can be eliminated without a change of meaning by using the operations of conversion, contraposition, or obversion on the statement containing non-A.

1. When conversion is applied to E-form and I-form statements, there is no change of meaning.

2. When contraposition is applied to A-form and O-form statements, there is no change of meaning.

3. When observation is applied to statements of any standard-form, there is no change of meaning.

Section 5.5: Ordinary Language Arguments

A. Again, many arguments that are not standard-form categorical syllogisms as written can be translated into standard-form syllogisms.

B. One technique for reducing the number of terms to three matched pairs is as follows: identify some factor common to two or all three propositions and then express this common factor through the strategic use of parameters.

1. For example, if all three statements are about people, then the term "people" or "people identical to" may be used. If all three statements are about times or places, the term "times" or "times identical to" or the term "places" or "places identical to" might be used.

2. Consider this example:

"Whenever people put off marriage until they are older, the divorce rate decreases. Today, people are putting off marriage until they are older. Therefore, the divorce rate is decreasing today."

3. This argument translates into the following standard-form categorical syllogism:

"All times people put off marriage until they are older are times the divorce rate decreases. All present times are times people put off marriage until they are older. Therefore, all present times are times the divorce rate decreases."

Section 5.6: Enthymemes

A. An enthymeme = df. an argument that is expressible as a categorical syllogism but the argument lacks a premise or a conclusion.

1. Enthymemes are common in spoken and written English.

2. The missing statement may be so obvious that it need not be conveyed. Alternatively, the speaker or writer may be trying to disguise a controversial, or false, statement.

B. The enthymeme should be converted into a syllogism, for the purpose of determining its validity or invalidity.

1. First, identify the missing premise or conclusion.

2. Second, with the aim of converting the enthymeme into a good argument, introduce the missing statement. Initially, the missing statement need not be expressed in categorical form.

3. Third, the entire argument may be translated into categorical form and then tested with a Venn diagram or by the rules for syllogisms.

Section 5.7: Sorites

A. In some cases two or more categorical syllogisms are combined in a chained series of arguments. In this chain there should be at least one intermediate conclusion which must function both as the conclusion of one syllogism and as the premise of another syllogism.

B. A sorites = df. a chain of categorical syllogisms without an intermediate conclusion that is needed to link two arguments of this chain.

1. Obviously, within a sorites there are two incomplete syllogisms.

2. To determine the validity of the syllogisms within a sorites, we must supply the intermediate conclusion in standard form.

C. The procedure for evaluating a sorites is as follows:

1. First, put the sorites into standard form.

2. Second, introduce the intermediate conclusions.

3. Third, test each component syllogism for validity.

D. A sorites is valid = df. each syllogism within a sorites forms a valid argument.

Chapter 6: Propositional Logic

Section 6.1: Propositional Logic

A. Validity and invalidity can be determined by the logical form of the argument.

1. This form can be conveyed within a symbolic language.

2. This symbolic language consists of some symbols to represent simple statements and other symbols to represent operators between simple statements.

B. **Simple statement** = df. statement that does not contain any other statement as a component.

1. For example, 'Butane is a hydrogen compound' is a simple statement.

2. Each simple statement is conveyed by an upper-case letter.

3. Each simple statement in logic must be true or false.

C. **Compound statement** = df. statement that contains at least one simple statement as a component. There are five types of compound statements, indicated in the following.

1. It is not the case that . . . .

2. If . . . , then . . . .

3. Either . . . or . . . .

4. . . . and . . . .

5. . . . if and only if . . . .

D. The negation compound statement. The first operator symbol is the negation sign, " ~ ", called "tilde".

1. The negation sign is used to negate any simple or compound statement.

a. "It is false that A."

b. "It is not the case that A."

c. "Not-A."

2. Use tilde, as in "$\sim$A", for a negation compound statement.

E. Conjunction compound statement. The second operator sign is the conjunction sign.

1. The dot "·" is used to translate many expressions conveying the meaning of 'and'.

2. This chart functions as a translation menu.

Natural Language Expression	Logical Form
A and B	A · B
A although B	"
A but B	"
A nevertheless B	"
Not only A, but also B	"
A whereas B	"
Despite A, B	"
A, however B	"

3. The conjunction statement is a compound statement that assumes 'and' between simple statements.

F. Disjunctive compound statement. The third operator sign is disjunctive sign, 'v'.

1. Notice the distinction between inclusive disjunction and exclusive disjunction.

a. Inclusive disjunction occurs when the "or" suggests that one or the other or possibly both simple statements are true.

(1) "In order to graduate each student must enroll in logic or they must enroll in math."

b. Exclusive disjunction occurs when the "or" means that one or the other but not both simple statements are true.

(1) "The train to New York will depart on track L or it will depart on track M."

2. The disjunctive sign, "v", conveys inclusive disjunction.

Chart

Natural Language Expression	Logical Form
A unless B	"
Either A or B	"

G. Conditional compound statement. The fourth operator sign is the horseshoe " ⊃ " used to translate "if. . . , then . . . ".

1. Within every conditional statement, the antecedent is the statement that appears after the word "if", and the consequent is the statement that appears after the word "then".

2. The "⊃" sign goes between the antecedent and the consequent.

3. The conditional statement means that some (consequent) statement is true under the assumption that some (antecedent) statement is true.

4. Chart

Natural Language Expression	Logical Form
If A, then B.	$A \supset B$
If A, B.	$A \supset B$
A, if B.	$B \supset A$
A, provided that B.	$B \supset A$
A, given that B.	$B \supset A$
A, in case B.	$B \supset A$
A implies B.	$A \supset B$
A entails B.	$A \supset B$
A only if B.	$A \supset B$
A is a necessary condition of B	$B \supset A$
A is a sufficient condition for B	$A \supset B$

5. Examples.

a. A only if B: "The car runs only if it has gasoline".

b. A is a necessary condition of B: "Having air to breath is a necessary condition of being alive".

c. A is a sufficient condition for B: "Achieving a score of '95' on the test is sufficient for passing the test".

H. Biconditional statement: The biconditional operator "$\equiv$" translates as "is equivalent to" or "if and only if".

1. Chart

<u>Natural Language Expression</u>	<u>Logical Form</u>
A if and only if B.	$A \equiv B$
A just in case B.	"
A is equivalent to B.	"
A is both necessary and sufficient for B.	"

2. Notice that the biconditional sign has a stronger meaning than the conditional sign: "$A \equiv B$" means "$(A \supset B) \cdot (B \supset A)$".

I. Translations

1. Parentheses or brackets are always needed when more than two letters are used within a compounded statement.

2. The statement "$A \cdot B \vee C$" is ambiguous, and therefore incorrect in this logical language.

a. This statement could mean '$(A \cdot B) \vee C$'.

b. Alternatively, the statement could mean '$A \cdot (B \vee C)$'.

3. The " $\sim$ " sign applies only to units that immediately follow it, except when parentheses or brackets are used.

a. $({\sim}A \vee B) \vee C$

b. ${\sim}(A \vee B) \vee C$

c. ${\sim}[(A \vee B) \vee C]$.

4. Chart

Natural Language Expression	Logical Form
Not both A and B.	$\sim(A \cdot B)$ or $\sim A \vee \sim B$
Both not A and not B.	$\sim A \cdot \sim B$ or $\sim(A \vee B)$
Neither A nor B.	$\sim(A \vee B)$ or $\sim A \cdot \sim B$

Section 6.2: Truth Functions of a Compound Statement

The principle of truth-functionality is as follows: the truth value of any compound statement is a function of the truth values of its components. The definition of every type of compound statement in propositional logic illustrates this principle.

A. Negation Statement: for any statement variable p, the negation of p, which is $\sim p$, will always have opposite truth value to p.

1. The statement variable p represents any statement whatsoever, even compound statements.

2. For each negation statement the main connective must be " $\sim$ ".

3. Again, the " $\sim$ " applies only to units that immediately follow it, except when parentheses or brackets are used. Which one of the following is a negation statement?

a. $(\sim A \vee B) \vee C$

b. $\sim(A \vee B) \vee C$

c. $\sim[(A \vee B) \vee C]$.

B. Conjunction statement: the statement form "$p \cdot q$" is true if and only if both p and q are true.

1. So, "A · B" is true just in case both A and B are true.

2. The main connective must be a dot.

C. Disjunctive statement: "p v q" is true if and only if either p or q (or both) is true.

1. "A v B" is true when either one or both disjuncts is true.

2. The main connective must be a wedge.

D. Conditional statement: the statement form "p ⊃ q" is false if and only if p is true and q is false. ("p ⊃ q" is true in all other cases.)

1. Truth-functional interpretation of the conditional statement relies solely on the truth values of the antecedent and the consequent.

a. "If it snows 10 feet tonight in the center of town, then the local high school will be closed tomorrow."

b. Assume that the antecedent is true and consequent is true. In such a case the conditional statement is true.

c. Assume that the antecedent is true and consequent false. In such a case the conditional statement is false.

d. Assume antecedent is false. In such a case the conditional is true, regardless of whether the consequent is true or false.

2. But there are many ridiculous statements, which are obviously false, that appear to be true according to the truth-function interpretation of the conditional statement.

a. "'If it snows 10 feet tonight in the center of town, then every student in this classroom has $1 billion in assets."

b. "If it snows 10 feet tonight in the center of town, then all bankers are Martians."

3. These examples illustrate the problem of counter-factual conditionals.

E. Biconditional statement: "p ≡ q" is true if and only if p and q have the same true value.

1. The biconditional statement is true whenever both p and q are true together or whenever they are false together.

2. "p ≡ q" is the same as "(p ⊃ q) · (q ⊃ p)".

<u>Section 6.3: Truth Tables for Propositions</u>

A. What is the goal of a truth table?

1. The major goal of a truth table is to show how the truth value of each compound statement depends directly on the truth values of the components of the compound statement.

2. Each truth table first gives all possible values to components of a compound statement, and then gives the truth value of the compound statement itself.

B. Construction of a truth table for "(A v ~B) ⊃ B".

1. How many lines to a truth table? Where n is the number of <u>different</u> components of a compound statement, the number of lines is 2^n.

2. Assign all possible combinations of t and f to A and to B.

3. Assign t and f to connective with smallest scope, then to connective with larger scope, etc.

C. Construction of truth table for "(A · ~B) ⊃ C".

1. Eight lines are needed for this truth table.

2. Assign all possible combinations of t and f to A and B.

3. Then assign t and f to connective with smallest scope, and then to connectives with larger scope, etc.

D. Classification of all compound statements in logic.

1. Tautologous statement = df. a compound statement which has all t's in its final column of the truth table. A tautology can never be false.

2. Self-contradictory statement = df. a compound statement which has all f's in its final column of the truth table. A self-contradiction can never be true.

3. Contingent statement = df. a compound statement which has at least one t and at least one f in its final column of the truth table. A contingent statement could be true or it could be false.

E. There are three types of logical relationships between two statements.

1. Logical equivalence between two statements.

a. Two statements are logically equivalent to each other if they have the same truth value on each line in the truth table, regardless of the truth values of the components.

b. "P ⊃ Q" is logically equivalent to "~Q ⊃ ~P".

2. Contradictory relationship

a. Two statements are contradictory of each other if they have opposite truth values in the truth table, regardless of the truth values of the components.

b. "P ⊃ Q" contradicts "P · ~Q".

3. Consistent relationship

a. Two statements are consistent with each other if there is at least one line in which both statements turn out to be true.

Section 6.4: Truth Table Method of Proving Validity or Invalidity

A. First, write out the symbolized argument on horizontal row.

1. Place a single slash between premises.

2. Place a double slash after premises and before conclusion.

B. Second, construct a truth table for entire argument.

C. Third, look for the line in which all true premises and the conclusion is false. If such a line is found, then and only then is the argument invalid.

D. Here are some unusual examples of using truth tables to prove validity.

1. Is the following argument valid: "S / ~S // P"? The answer is "yes", because any argument with contradictory premises is valid, regardless of the conclusion.

2. Is the following argument valid: "S // R v ~R"? The answer is "yes", because any argument with a tautologous conclusion is valid, regardless of the conclusion.

Section 6.5: Indirect Truth Tables for Arguments

A. In addition to the method of proving validity/invalidity by truth tables as depicted in Section 6.4, a shorter and faster method involves indirect truth tables.

B. Indirect truth tables are constructed from the following steps:

1. First, write the symbolized argument on a single line, placing a single slash

between the premises and a double slash between the last premise and the conclusion.

2. Second, assume that all the premises are true and the conclusion false.

a. To do this write 'T' under the main connective of each premise, and write 'F' under the main connective of the conclusion.

b. For example,

A ⊃ (B v C) / B ⊃ D / A // ~C ⊃ D

T T T F

3. Third, calculate the truth-values of all the separate components of the premises and conclusion.

a. This calculation should end by a truth-value assignment to each atomic letter of the argument.

b. For example,

A ⊃ (B v C) / B ⊃ D / A // ~C ⊃ D

T T F F F F T F T T F F F

4. Fourth, determine whether or not a contradiction appears anywhere within the calculation of truth values to the argument. A contradiction arises when both "T" and "F" are assigned to any atomic letter or compound statement within the argument.

a. If a contradiction does arise, then the assumption of step 2 above, that all premises are true and conclusion false, cannot be true.

(1) In such a case it is impossible for all premises to be true and conclusion false; this of course means that the argument is <u>valid</u>.

(2) For example, the contradiction arises within the first

premise.

A ⊃ (B v C) / B ⊃ D / A // ~C ⊃ D

T T F F F   F T F   T   T F F F

b. On the other hand, if a contradiction does not arise after a complete assignment of truth values to all atomic letters and components of the statements, then the assumption of step 2 above can be true.

(1)In such a case it is possible for all premises to be true and conclusion false; this of course means that the argument is invalid.

(2) For example, no contradiction arises in the following argument:

~A ⊃ (B v C) / ~B // C ⊃ A

TF T F T T   TF   T F F

Section 6.6: Argument Forms and Fallacies

A. What are the logical properties common to these arguments?

T v M	C v (D · E)	(A ⊃ B) v ~(C · D)
~T/	~C/	~(A ⊃ B)/
M	D · E	~(C · D)

B. These properties can be depicted by an argument form.

1. Argument form = df. an arrangement of statement variables and operators such that the uniform replacement of the variables by statements results in an argument. The argument is called the substitution instance of the argument form.

a. Variable = df. a symbol that represents any statement whatsoever, either simple or compound.

b. Every argument form must conform to the following rule: every operator symbol that appears in the argument form must also appear in the argument; but it is not true that every connective symbol in the argument must appear in its argument form.

2. The argument form for the three arguments above is as follows:

a. p v q

~p /

q

b. Another example of this form:

~A v [(M ⊃ N) v O]

~ ~A /

(M ⊃ N) v O

3. A valid argument form = df. an argument form which has only valid arguments as its substitution instances. An invalid argument form has at least one invalid argument as a substitution instance.

a. An example of a valid argument form is disjunctive syllogism:

p v q

~p /

q

b. An example of an invalid argument form is:

p

q /

r

C. Additional valid argument forms.

1. Modus Ponens (MP)

$p \supset q$

p /

q.

2. Constructive Dilemma (CD)

$(p \supset q) \cdot (r \supset s)$

p v r /

q v s

3. Modus Tollens (MT)

$p \supset q$

~q /

~p.

4. Pure Hypothetical Syllogism (HS)

$p \supset q$

$q \supset r$ /

$p \supset r$.

D. Two invalid argument forms are as follow:

1. Affirming the Consequent (AC)

$p \supset q$

q /

p.

2. Denying the Antecedent (DA)

$p \supset q$

$\sim p$ /

$\sim q$.

Chapter 7: Natural Deduction in Propositional Logic

Section 7.1: Rules of Implication I

A. Let us consider four important valid argument forms.

1. Modus ponens (MP): Assume that one premise is a conditional statement and another premise is the antecedent of the conditional statement; we may conclude that the consequent is true.

$$p \supset q$$

$$p \; /$$

$$q.$$

2. Modus tollens (MT): Assume that one premise is a conditional statement, but another premise states that the consequent is false; we may infer in the conclusion that the antecedent is false.

$$p \supset q$$

$$\sim q \; /$$

$$\sim p.$$

3. Hypothetical syllogism (HS): Two conditional statements, as premises, can lead to a conditional statement in the conclusion.

$$p \supset q$$

$$q \supset r \; /$$

$$p \supset r.$$

4. Disjunctive syllogism (DS): Assume that the premises contain a disjunction of two alternatives and that the first alternative is negated; we may conclude that the other alternative is true.

p v q

~p /

q.

B. Natural deduction is a method of proving validity by using some combination of valid argument forms.

1. The proof itself is broken down into a certain number of steps (inferences). Each step comprises a substitution instance of some valid argument form.

2. The particular sequence of steps that are needed within a proof never follows a pre-arranged, fixed pattern. So, one can never tell in advance which valid forms will be needed. Consider this example:

1. F v (D ⊃ T)

2. ~F

3. D / T

4. D ⊃ T 1, 2 DS

5. T 3,4 MP

3. Steps in writing a proof:

a. List and number premises.

b. To right of last premise, write " / " and the conclusion.

c. Number each inferred statements.

d. Justify each inferred statement by writing the number of the previous steps needed and the rule.

Section 7.2: Rules of Implication II

A. Constructive Dilemma (CD):

$(p \supset q) \cdot (r \supset s)$

$p \vee s$ /

$q \vee s$

B. Simplification (Simp)

$p \cdot q$ /

p

C. Conjunction (Conj)

p

q /

$p \cdot q$

D. Addition (Add)

p /

$p \vee q$

Section 7.3: Rules of Replacement I

A. **Axiom of replacement** = df. in the context of a proof, logically equivalent expressions may replace one another, even within a segment of a compound statement.

1. Rules of replacement are not rules of validity. A rule of replacement permits the substitution of one statement for another equivalent statement.

2. <u>Each rule of replacement can apply to an entire line, or to any segment of a</u>

line. Conversely, a rule of validity cannot be applied to a segment of a line.

B. Rules of replacement

1. DeMorgan's Rule: When moving a tilde inside or outside a set of parentheses, a dot switches with a wedge and conversely.

$$\sim(p \cdot q) :: (\sim p \vee \sim q)$$

$$\sim(p \vee q) :: (\sim p \cdot \sim q)$$

2. Commutativity (Com):

$(p \vee q) :: (q \vee p)$

$(p \cdot q) :: (q \cdot p)$

3. Associativity (Assoc):

$p \vee (q \vee r)] :: [(p \vee q) \vee r]$

$[p \cdot (q \cdot r)] :: [(p \cdot q) \cdot r]$

4. Distribution (Dist):

$[p \cdot (q \vee r)] :: [(p \cdot q) \vee (p \cdot r)]$

$[p \vee (q \cdot r)] :: [(p \vee q) \cdot (p \vee r)]$

5. Double Negation (DN):

$p :: \sim\sim p$

Section 7.4: Rules of Replacement II

A. Transposition (Trans):

$(p \supset q) :: (\sim q \supset \sim p)$

B. Material Implication (Imp):

$(p \supset q) :: (\sim p \vee q)$

C. Material equivalence (Equiv):

$(p \equiv q) :: [(p \supset q) \cdot (q \supset p)]$

$(p \equiv q) :: [(p \cdot q) \vee (\sim p \cdot \sim q)]$

D. Exportation (Exp):

$[(p \cdot q) \supset r] :: [p \supset (q \supset r)]$

E. Tautology (Taut):

$p :: (p \vee p)$

$p :: (p \cdot p)$

F. General strategies for proofs.

1. Divide and conquer by breaking up long statements in the premises. See Exercise 7.4, II, #23.

2. The rule of material implication is frequently used to convert all conditional statements to disjunctions, which promote the use of the rule of distribution. Material implication is also used to convert all disjunctions to conditional statements, which promotes the use of hypothetical syllogism. See Exercise 7.4, II, #27, #29.

3. Work "from the top down" by examining the logical structure of each premise and then determining what rule could possibly be used as the first rule of the proof. This is very much a trial and error process. Here are some examples:

a. #7 "$M \supset (U \supset H)$" permits Exportation.

b. #19 "$I \vee (N \cdot F)$" permits Distribution.

4. Work "from the bottom up" by examining the logical structure of the

conclusion and then determining what rule is likely to be used as the last rule of the proof in deriving the conclusion. This is very much a trial and error process.

a. From #11, derive a single letter conclusion from the rule of tautology.

b. See #2, using DeMorgan at the end.

__Section 7.5: Conditional Proof__

A. Conditional proof is a method for proving a particular statement, which is usually a conditional statement. In some cases conditional proof is both shorter and simpler to use than the direct method of proof presented in section 7.1 through 7.4.

B. Steps of a conditional proof. Imagine that we are trying to prove a conditional statement, such as "A ⊃ E".

1. First, the conditional proof begins by indenting a line which consists of the antecedent "A" of the conditional statement "A ⊃ E". This line is justified by "ACP", referring to "assumption for conditional proof".

2. Second, apply the ordinary rules of inference and equivalence to any previous line in the proof in a series of lines including the ACP line, in a series of indented lines. The purpose of this application is the derivation of the consequent "E" of "A ⊃ E".

3. Third, discharge the conditional sequence in a conditional statement "A ⊃ E" that is not indented. Justify this statement by referring to the sequence of numbers of the lines within the conditional proof, and by "CP" referring to "conditional proof".

C. However, there is an important restriction in using conditional proof: after the proof has been discharged, no line that appeared within the sequence of the conditional proof may be used as a reason for a subsequent line in the remainder of the proof.

D. This method of conditional proof may be used to derive a conditional statement appearing anywhere within the proof, and not only as the conclusion of the argument. Also, one conditional sequence may appear within another conditional sequence.

Section 7.6: Indirect Proof

A. In addition to conditional proof, indirect proof is also a method for proving either the conclusion or some intermediate line leading to the conclusion.

B. Steps of an indirect proof.

1. First, assume the negation of the statement (either conclusion or some other line) you are intending to prove. This negated statement should be indented and justified by "AIP", referring to "assumption for indirect proof".

2. Second, derive any self-contradictory statement (a logical falsehood) by applying the rules of validity and equivalence to the lines above the assumption for indirect proof, the AIP.

a. A "sub-proof" is indented and included within the main proof.

b. The self-contradictory statement ends this sub-proof. This statement need not include any atomic component of the AIP, since any logical falsehood will be sufficient here.

3. Third, complete the indirect proof by concluding that the original assumption, the AIP, is false in a line that is not indented. This is justified by IP, referring

to indirect proof together with the numerals indicating all indented lines of this proof.

C. However, there is an important restriction in using indirect proof: after the proof has been discharged, no line that appeared within the indented sequence of the indirect proof can be used as a reason for a subsequent line in the remainder of the proof.

D. The method of indirect proof may be combined with conditional proof. This is accomplished by including indirect proof within condition proof, or conversely including conditional proof within indirect proof.

Section 7.7: Proving Logical Truths

A. The two methods of conditional proof and indirect proof are quite useful in proving a tautology, which is a logically true statement.

B. If the tautology being proven is a conditional statement, then the method of conditional proof may be quite helpful.

1. First, assume the antecedent of this conditional, and justify this assumption by ACP, assumption of conditional proof.

2. Second, derive the consequent of this conditional by applying the eighteen rules of validity and equivalence to all lines above ACP.

3. Third, discharge the proof by writing the conditional statement itself, justified by CP, conditional proof. The same restrictions on flexibility we saw for conditional proof from Section 7.5 apply here as well.

C. Indirect proofs are typically used for statements that are not conditional statements.

1. First, assume the negation of the statement being proven, based on the

assumption of indirect proof, which is called "AIP".

2. Second, derive any self-contradictory statement by applying the rule of validity and equivalence within an indented sequence of proof.

3. Third, discharge the indirect proof by writing the statement being proven, justified by IP, referring to indirect proof. Again, the same restrictions on flexibility of indirect proof from Section 7.6 apply here as well.

D. Again, these methods of indirect proof and conditional proof may be combined by including one method within the other method. In other words, an indirect proof may be constructed within a conditional proof, and vice versa.

Chapter 8: Predicate Logic

Section 8.1: Predicate Logic

A. In this course there are three systems for translating ordinary language arguments into logical symbols: propositional logic, categorical logic, and predicate logic.

1. Propositional logic assumes that the smallest unit of logical analysis is the whole simple statement.

a. For example,

"If A, then B.

If B, then C.

Therefore, if A, then C."

b. The letters "A", "B", and "C" each represents whole statements, either singular or compound.

c. Validity of the argument does not depend on anything smaller than the simple statement.

2. Categorical logic assumes that the subject term and the predicate term are the smallest units of analysis.

a. For example,

"All insurance policies are cryptically written documents. Therefore, some insurance policies are cryptically written documents."

b. Within categorical logic the methods for proving validity do not rely on rules from propositional logic.

3. Predicate logic combines aspects from both propositional logic and

categorical logic.

a. From categorical logic the smallest units of analysis are subject terms and predicate terms.

b. From propositional logic the rules for combining entire statements are applied.

c. So, in predicate logic validity depends on both the arrangement of terms and the logical relationships between statements.

B. Predicate logic can be used to translate three important kinds of statements: singular, universal, and particular statements.

C. What is a singular statement?

1. A singular statement = df. a statement that asserts that one or more specifically named entity has, or does not have, a property.

2. The entity can be any object, place, thing, or time.

3. There are two components of every singular statement, identified as the predicate and the subject.

a. First, a predicate conveys the meaning that "____ is or is not some property".

(1) Each predicate is symbolized by a capital letter, A, B, . . Z.

(2) "_____ is happy" translates as "H__".

b. Second, a subject is that which is attributed with a property by the predicate.

(1)Each subject is symbolized by an individual constant,

represented by lower case letters, from the sequence a to w.

(2) Each individual constant names an existing individual, thing, or person.

(3) "George ____" translates as "__ g".

c. "George is pig" translates as "Pg".

4. A compound arrangement of singular statements follows the rules of propositional logic, defining the ~, · , v, ⊃, and ≡.

D. What is a universal statement?

1. A universal statement = df. a statement that asserts that every unspecified member of a class has, or does not have, a property.

a. Example #1: "All skyscrapers are tall."

b. Example #2: "All ambassadors are nervous."

c. Example #3: "No frogs are birds."

d. Example #4: "No diamonds are ugly."

2. What is a Boolean interpretation of a universal affirmative statement?

a. First formulation from ordinary language:

"All skyscrapers are tall."

b. Second formulation from Boolean logic:

"For any thing in our universe of discourse,

if it is a skyscraper, then it is tall."

c. Third formulation with symbols:

"For any x, if x is S then x is T."

(1) S and T are predicates.

(2) This formulation includes an "if-then" statement.

(3) The phrase "For any x" is new up to this point in our study. It refers to each and every member of our universe of discourse. "For any x" is a universal quantifier, which governs everything following it.

d. Fourth formulation from predicate logic:

"(x) (Sx ⊃ Tx)"

(1) "(x)" = "For any x" = "For anything in our universe of discourse. . . ".

3. What is the Boolean interpretation of a universal negative statement?

a. First formulation from ordinary language:

"No frogs are birds."

b. Second formulation from Boolean interpretation:

"For anything in our universe of discourse,

if it is a frog, then it is not a bird."

c. Third formulation with symbols:

"For any x, if x is F then x is not B."

(1) "For any x" is again a universal quantifier which governs everything that follows it, which in this case is the set of all frogs.

(2) "For any x" = df. "(x)".

d. Fourth formulation from predicate logic:

"(x) (Fx ⊃ ~Bx)"

E. What is a particular statement?

1. A particular statement = df. a statement that asserts that at least one <u>unspecified</u> member of a class has, or does not have, a property.

2. Examples

a. "Some men are paupers."

b. "Some diseases are not contagious."

c. "Some jobs are boring."

d. "Some vehicles are not motorcycles."

3. What is the Boolean interpretation of a particular affirmative statement?

a. First formulation from ordinary language:

"Some men are paupers."

b. Second formulation from Boolean logic:

"There is at least one thing in the universe which is a man, and this thing is also a pauper."

c. Third formulation with symbols:

"There exists an x such that x is an M and x is a P."

(1) This statement assumes the existence of at least one thing with two properties, designated by "M" and "P".

(2) Within this formulation there is a conjunction with two predicates.

d. Fourth formulation from predicate logic: "$(\exists x)\ (Mx \cdot Px)$"

(1) "$(\exists x)$" means "there exists an x such that".

(2) "$(\exists x)$" is called an existential quantifier.

(3) This formulation requires existence of at least one thing with these predicates.

4. How should we translate a negation of a particular statement?

a. First formulation: "Some vehicles are not motorcycles."

b. Second formulation: "There is at least one thing in the universe which is a vehicle and is not a motorcycle."

c. Third formulation: "There exists an x such that x is a V and x is not M."

d. Fourth formulation: "$(\exists x)\ (Vx \cdot \sim Mx)$".

E. Guidelines for translating statements into predicate logic.

1. First, if a statement is compound, then write down the main connective.

2. Second, for each grammatically simple statement, determine what type of statement it is.

a. Singular statement (for example, "The White House is not pink.")

(1) Symbolize each predicate with a capital letter.

(2) Symbolize each subject with lower-case letter.

b. Universal statement (for example, "All houses in this town are buildings with two floors.")

c. Particular statement (for example, "Some houses in this town are buildings with two floors.")

3. Negation statements

a. "No doctor is poor" translates as "(x) (Dx ⊃ ~Px)".

b. "No student has graduated" translates as "(x)(Sx ⊃ ~Gx)".

c. "It is not the case that every doctor is poor" translates as "~(x) (Dx ⊃ Px)". This statement is equivalent to "(∃x)(Dx · ~Px)".

d. "It is not the case that all students have graduated" translates as "~(x) (Sx ⊃ Gx)". This statement is equivalent to "(∃x)(Sx · ~Gx)".

4. Some statements include the expressions "only" or "none but".

a. "Only close friends were invited" translates as

"(x) (Ix ⊃ Cx)".

b. "None but citizens are voters" translates as

"(x) (Vx ⊃ Cx)".

F. Translation Menu:

Statement	Logical Form
Any A is a B.	(x)(Ax ⊃ Bx)
A few A's are B's.	(∃x)(Ax · Bx)
Only A's are B's.	(x)(Bx ⊃ Ax)
None but A's are B's.	(x)(Bx ⊃ Ax)
It is not the case that all A's are B's.	~(x)(Ax ⊃ Bx)
	(∃x)(Ax · ~Bx)

Not any A's are B's. $(x)(Ax \supset \sim Bx)$

$\sim(\exists x)(Ax \cdot Bx)$

If some A's are B's, then all D's are E's. $(\exists x)(Ax \cdot Bx) \supset (x)(Dx \supset Ex)$

All A's and all B's are both C and D. $(x)[(Ax \vee Bx) \supset (Cx \cdot Dx)]$

All things that are both A and B are C and D. $(x)[(Ax \cdot Bx) \supset (Cx \cdot Dx)]$

Section 8.2: Removing and Introducing Quantifiers

A. The first 8 rules of validity from sections 7.1 and 7.2 cannot apply to quantification arguments.

1. Consider this valid argument:

$(x)(Cx \supset Sx)$

Cm / Sm.

2. We need rules to remove quantifiers, and rules to introduce quantifiers.

3. These new rules must apply to whole lines within a proof, and can never apply to portions of a line.

B. Universal instantiation is an operation that provides an instance of the universal statement, such as "$(x)(Cx \supset Sx)$". There are two formulations of universal instantiation.

1. First formulation of universal instantiation: universal instantiation directs us to delete a quantifier and then to replace every variable within that quantifier with the same individual constant.

a. Rule:

From: $(x)\beta x$ (where β represents any predicate letter.)

To: ßa.

b. The premise must be a universal statement. But, there is no restriction on which individual constant appears in the conclusion, so long as consistency is preserved.

c. Example of valid argument from above:

1. (x) (Cx ⊃ Sx)

2. Cm / Sm.

3. Cm ⊃ Sm 1 UI

4. Sm 2,3 MP

2. Second formulation of universal instantiation: universal instantiation directs us to delete a quantifier and then to use the same (or different) variable within a statement function.

a. Rule: From: (x)ßx (or any other variable)

To: ßx (or any other variable).

b. There is no restriction on the selection of the variables in the conclusion, as long as consistency is preserved.

c. The difference between the first and second formulations of universal instantiation is as follows: in the first formulation the inferred line must include an individual constant, but in the second formulation the inferred lines must include a variable.

d. However, no argument in predicate logic can end with a conclusion like "ßx", because this cannot be translated into a meaningful statement.

e. Consider this valid argument:

1. (x)(Px ⊃ Dx)

2. (x)(Dx ⊃ Cx) / (x)(Px ⊃ Cx)

3. Py ⊃ Dy 1 UI

4. Dy ⊃ Cy 2 UI

C. Universal generalization directs us to infer a universal generalization from a statement function. This rule reintroduces a universal quantifier from a statement function which lacks a universal quantifier.

1. Consider this example:

a. "Dy ⊃ Cy" from statement #4 above is a statement function.

b. We can infer "(x)(Dx ⊃ Cx)" by universal generalization. The particular variable selected is irrelevant, as long as the variable is the same throughout the statement.

2. Rule: From: ßy (or any other variable)

To: (x)ßx (or any other variable).

3. The premise, "ßy", may contain any variable but cannot contain an individual constant, such as in "Fa".

4. Here is an example.

1. (x)(Px ⊃ Dx)

2. (x)(Dx ⊃ Cx) / (x)(Px ⊃ Cx)

3. Py ⊃ Dy 1 UI

4. Dy ⊃ Cy 2 UI

5. $Py \supset Cy$ 3,4 HS

6. $(x)(Px \supset Cx)$ 5 UG

D. Existential generalization is used to reintroduce an existential quantifier. There are two formulations of existential generalization.

1. The first formulation reintroduces an existential quantifier from a singular statement:

a. For example,

From: "Sp"

To: "$(\exists x)Sx$"

b. Rule: From: ßa (or any other constant)

To: $(\exists x)$ßx (or any other variable)

c. Let us apply this rule to an argument:

1. $(x)(Cx \supset Sx)$

2. Cp / $(\exists x)Sx$

3. $Cp \supset Sp$ 1 UI

4. Sp 2,3 MP

5. $(\exists x)Sx$ 4 EG

2. The second formulation of existential generalization reintroduces an existential quantifier from a statement function.

a. For example:

From: "Qy"

To: "$(\exists x)Qx$".

b. Rule: From: ßy (or any other variable)

To: (∃x)ßx (or any other variable).

c. The difference between the first and second formulations of existential generalization is as follows: in the first formulation the rule is applied to a singular statement, but in the second formulation the rule is applied to a statement function.

E. Existential instantiation provides an instance of an existential quantification by giving the "something" in the existential quantification a new name. This rule removes an existential quantifier and provides a new name (an individual constant).

1. For example

From: (∃x)(Ax · Gx)

To: Ad · Gd

2. Rule: From: (∃x)ßx (or any other variable)

To: ßa.

3. This rule includes an important restriction:

a. According to this rule, the selection of a particular individual constant, such as "a" in the rule above, is somewhat arbitrary.

b. The restriction in using this rule is that the individual constant must not appear in any line above "ßa", and that the individual constant must not appear in the conclusion. However, the constant may appear in lines below the "ßa", except for the conclusion.

F. Suggestions for proofs

1. Always try to break-up a compound statement that include quantifiers. This

step is needed because we cannot remove the quantifiers from compound statements. See Exercise 8.2, I, #12, #13.

2. Always try to remove quantifiers from existential generalizations and universal generalization. When the premises include one of each, apply existential instantiation prior to universal instantiation. See Exercise 8.2, I, #7, #11

3. Once all quantifiers are removed, apply the 18 rules from Chapter 7.

4. If the conclusion is an existential statement, then think of the rule existential generalization as the last step. See Exercise 8.2, I, #6, #7, 11, 13. A similar sequence applies for a conclusion that is a universal statement, as in Exercise 8.2, I, #10, #14

Section 8.3: Change of Quantifier Rules

A. In order to prove the validity for many arguments in predicate logic, we need rules for removing those negation signs that precede the quantifiers.

1. Existential instantiation cannot be applied to the following:

" ~(∃x)(Px · ~Qx)".

2. Universal instantiation cannot be applied to the following:

" ~(x)(~Rx v Qx)".

B. Consider the following two equivalent statements: "It is not the case that everything in the universe is solid" and "Something is not solid".

1. These two equivalent statements illustrate the following rules of equivalence.

a. ~(x)Sx :: (∃x)~Sx

b. $\sim(\exists x)Sx :: (x)\sim Sx$

2. In these rules we can replace '$\sim Sx$' for 'Sx'.

a. $\sim(x)\sim Sx :: (\exists x)Sx$

b. $\sim(\exists x)\sim Sx :: (x)Sx$

C. Here are four rules permitting a change of a quantifier:

1. $(x)\beta x :: \sim(\exists x)\sim\beta x$

2. $\sim(x)\beta x :: (\exists x)\sim\beta x$

3. $(\exists x)\beta x :: \sim(x)\sim\beta x$

4. $\sim(\exists x)\beta x :: (x)\sim\beta x$

D. Since these rules are stated as logical equivalences, they apply to parts of lines as well as to whole lines.

Section 8.4: Conditional and Indirect Proof

A. The technique of conditional proof can be used for certain arguments with conclusions expressed in the form of conditional statements or disjunctions.

1. Step #1: assume the antecedent of the conditional statement to be obtained, as the first line of an indented sequence.

2. Step #2: derive the consequent of the conditional statement to be obtained, as the last line of an indented sequence. This derivation must, of course, conform to all the rules of inference and equivalence from Chapters 7 and 8, up to this point.

3. Step #3: discharge the conditional sequence in a conditional statement that exactly matches the one to be obtained.

4. There is a restriction to the use of conditional proof: universal generalization must not be used within the scope of an indented sequence, if the instantial variable occurs freely in the first line of that sequence.

B. Indirect proof.

1. Step #1: assume the negation of the statement to be obtained, as the first line of an indented sequence.

2. Step #2: derive any self-contradictory statement, as the last line of an indented sequence. This derivation must, of course, conform to all the rules of inference and equivalence from Chapters 7 and 8, up to this point.

3. Step #3: discharge the indirect sequence by asserting the negation of the assumption made from Step #1.

C. A conditional proof sequence may be included with an indirect proof sequence, and <u>vice versa</u>.

<u>Section 8.5: Proving Invalidity</u>

A. The method of natural deduction in predicate logic (Section 8.2) cannot prove invalidity of an argument. But the counterexample method, introduced in Chapter 1 above, can. The counterexample method includes the following steps.

1. First, isolate the logical form of the argument. Here is the logical form of an argument expressed within the language of predicate logic:

$(\exists x)(Ax \cdot \sim Bx)$

$(x)(Cx \supset Bx)$ /

$(\exists x)(Cx \cdot \sim Ax)$

2. Second, construct another argument as a substitution instance of this form having all true premises and a false conclusion. Any substitution instance of this form is constructed by replacing the predicate letters with descriptive words.

a. For example,

"Some animals are not mammals.

All dogs are animals.

Therefore, some dogs are not mammals."

b. This argument is a substitution instance of the logical form stated above, and has all true premises and a false conclusion. Clearly, this argument is invalid.

3. Since this argument is an invalid instance of the form, it follows that the form is also invalid.

B. Another method for proving invalidity in predicate logic is the finite universe method.

1. To test for the invalidity of the argument, assume that the universe of discourse consists of only one object. Then, apply the method of indirect truth table from Section 6.5. If it is possible for premises to be true and the conclusion false in this universe, then the argument is identified as invalid.

2. Within the argument translate each particular statement and each universal statement into a singular statement. This is done by imagining that the entire universe of discourse consists of only one named thing, and then creating a singular statement with respect to that thing as the subject.

a. Assume that the universe consists only of Abigail. In such a case "(x)Px" implies "Pa", and "(∃x)Px" also implies "Pa".

b. Repeat this same translation procedure for a universe consisting of two members, and then three members.

3. If it is not possible for the premises to be true and the conclusion false, then test for invalidity of the argument by indirect truth table. But this time assume two objects in the universe. If it is possible for premises to be true and the conclusion false in this universe, then the argument is identified as invalid.

4. Otherwise, test again for invalidity by indirect truth table assuming three objects in the universe. Keep repeating this test for universes of increasing size until invalidity can be proven.

Section 8.6: Relational Predicates and Overlapping Quantifiers

A. Two types of predicates are possible within predicate logic.

1. Monadic predicates are one-place predicates. These have been the only type of predicates used up to this point in Chapter 8.

a. For each monadic predicate an attribute is assigned to a single thing or a single class of things.

b. For example, in "Some dogs have fleas" the predicate "has fleas" is monadic because the attribute of having fleas is assigned to members of the single class of dogs.

2. A relational predicate, which is the subject of Section 8.6, is a many-place

predicate.

a. For each relational predicate a relation is assigned between or among more than one thing, or more than one class of things.

b. The predicate ". . . is to the right of . . . " is a binary relation because it establishes a connection between two individuals. The predicate ". . . is between . . . and . . . " is a trinary relation, establishing a connection between three things.

c. Each relational predicate establishes an n-ary relation between n things, or between n classes of things, where n is greater than 1.

B. Each relational predicate is translated just like monadic predicates, except that for relational predicates two or more lower case letters are written after the upper-case letter representing the relation.

1. Consider two types of singular statements.

a. First, "My dog Rusty has fleas" is translated as "Fr".

b. Second, "My dog Rusty is heavier than my dog Pepper" is translated as "Hrp". Notice the two-place predicate ". . . is heavier than . . . ".

2. Consider three types of universal statements.

a. "All dogs are hairy" is translated as "(x)(Dx ⊃ Hx)", with a monadic predicate ". . . is (are) hairy".

b. "Thomas knows everything" is translated as "(x)Ktx" with the two-place predicate ". . . knows . . . ".

c. "All dogs are taller than all ants" is translated as "(x)(y)[(Dx · Ay) ⊃ Txy]".

(1) This example has overlapping quantifiers, represented by "(x)(y)" which translates as "For any x and for any y . . . ".

(2) Universal quantifiers that appear adjacent to each other in this way are overlapping. The sequence of overlapping universal quantifiers is irrelevant: "(x)(y)" is equivalent to "(y)(x)".

3. Consider three types of existential statements.

a. "Some dogs are tall" is translated as "(∃x)(Dx · Tx)" with the monadic predicate ". . . is tall".

b. "Thomas knows something" is translated as "(∃x)Ktx" with the two place predicate ". . . knows . . . ".

c. "Some person knows something" translates as "(∃x)(∃y)Kxy" with the same two-place predicate ". . . knows . . . ".

(1) This example also illustrates overlapping quantifiers, in this case involving two existential quantifiers.

(2) Again, since the quantifiers are both existential, the sequence is irrelevant. That is, "(∃x)(∃y)" is equivalent to "(∃y)(∃x)".

C. What happens when the overlapping quantifiers are different from one another?

1. In such a case it is important to determine whether an existential quantifier precedes a universal quantifier, or <u>vice versa</u>. This is because "(∃x)(y)" is rarely equivalent to "(y)(∃x)".

2. Notice that for any statement in predicate logic every variable must be bound by some quantifier, either existential or universal. Also, the particular variable used in

the predicate must be the same variable appearing in its associated binding quantifier.

Section 8.7: Identity

A. Many statements in ordinary language involve a special relation called identity, which is translated by the equal sign, " = ". Consider a few types of identity statements.

B. Some identity statements are called simple identity statements, which by definition assert that a named individual is identical to another named individual.

1. To translate a simple identity statement, write the equal sign, " = ", between two lower case letters, each of which represents a named individual.

a. For example, "Samuel Clemens is Mark Twain" translates as "c = t".

2. A negated identity statement asserts that a named individual is not identical to another named individual.

a. This negated identity relation is translated by drawing a slash through the identity symbol, " ≠ ".

b. For example, "William Wordsworth is not John Keats" translates as "w ≠ k".

4. To simplify the translation of lengthy strings of conjunctions, we may drop parentheses when the conjunction sign controls only the letters to its immediate left and right. Similarly, since the identity relation controls only letters to its immediate left and right, we may drop parentheses around an identity statement within a longer compound statement.

C. Identity relations are also useful in translating "Only," "The Only," and "No . . .

except", when the term that follows these phrases is an individual thing or person.

1. "Only Nixon resigned the presidency" obviously has "Nixon" following the term "only". This statement can be broken into two parts.

a. First, "Nixon resigned the presidency" translates as "Pn".

b. Second, "if anyone resigned the presidency, that person is Nixon" translates as "(x)(Px ⊃ x = n)".

c. The complete translation is "Pn · (x)(Px ⊃ x = n)".

2. "The only opera written by Beethoven is Fidelio" translates as "Of · Bf · (x)[(Ox · Bx) ⊃ x = f]".

3. "No nation except Australia is a continent" translates as "Na · Ca · (x)[(Nx · Cx) ⊃ x = a]".

D. Identity relations can be useful in translating "All . . . except. . . ".

1. "All presidents except Washington had a predecessor" translates into two parts.

2. First, "Washington did not have a predecessor" translates as " ~Rw ", where R refers to having a predecessor.

3. Second, "All presidents other than Washington did have a predecessor" translates as "(x)[(Px · x ≠ w) ⊃ Rx]".

4. Combining these two parts, the statement above is translated as " ~Rw · (x)[(Px · x ≠ w) ⊃ Rx]".

E. Numerical Statements

1. We can use a universal quantifier with an identity relation to assert that at

most n items have a certain property.

a. For example, consider "There is at most one U.S. Representative from Alaska".

b. This statement translates as "$(x)(y)[(Ux \cdot Ax \cdot Uy \cdot Ay) \supset x = y]$".

2. We can use an existential quantifier to assert that at least n items have a certain property.

a. For example, "There are at least two women in Hamlet." translates as "$(\exists x)(\exists y)(Wx \cdot Hx \cdot Wy \cdot Hy \cdot x \neq y)$".

3. A statement about exactly n items requires both a statement about at least n items and a statement about at most n items.

a. "There is exactly one city in Grenada" translates as "$(\exists x)\{Cx \cdot Gx \cdot (y)[(Cy \cdot Gy) \supset x = y]\}$".

F. Definite Descriptions

1. A definite description is roughly a statement identifying an individual person, place, or thing without specifically naming that person, place, or thing.

2. A definite description asserts three things: an item of a certain sort exists, there is only one such item, and that item has the attribute assigned to it by the statement.

3. For example, "The inventor of the phonograph was an American" means "There is someone who invented the phonograph, and if anyone invented the phonograph then that person is identical to the first, and the first person is an American".

4. This statement translates as "$(\exists x)[Ixp \cdot (y)(Iyp \supset y = x) \cdot Ax]$".

Chapter 9: Induction

Section 9.1: Analogy and Legal and Moral Reasoning

A. Analogical reasoning underlies many arguments within everyday judgments and decisions. Such reasoning is always inductive.

1. Analogical reasoning is reasoning based on an analogical comparison between two subjects, such as events, entities, or ideas. Every analogy requires that there are known similarities, known differences, and unknown relations between the two subjects in question.

2. When such reasoning is expressed as an argument, the result is an argument from analogy.

B. Simple arguments from analogy have the following structure:

Subject A_1 has attributes f, g, h, . . ., and z.

Subject A_2 has attributes f, g, h, . . ., and z.

.

.

Subject A_j has attributes f, g, h, . . ., and z.

Subject B has attributes f, g, h.

Therefore, subject B probably has attribute z also.

1. From this structure the subjects A_1 through A_j are called the primary analogates, and the subject B is called the secondary analogate.

2. Attributes f, g, h are the known similarities between the primary analogates and the secondary analogate. The conclusion states that z is probably an attribute of B.

C. The criteria for determining the success or failure of an argument by analogy are not precise. No single criterion can function as a necessary requirement or a sufficient condition for the success of the argument from analogy. Yet some of the "imprecise" criteria are as follows:

1. The known similarities between primary and secondary analogates should be relevant towards demonstrating the fact that B probably has attribute z.

2. The strength of the argument from analogy is dependent on the number of known similarities between primary analogates and secondary analogate.

3. The known differences between primary analogates and secondary analogate should not weaken the connection between premises and conclusion.

4. The argument from analogy is strengthened with a greater number of primary analogates, indicated by A_k above, that display the known similarities to the secondary analogate.

5. The primary analogates should be relatively diverse.

6. The argument from analogy is weakened as the attribute z is more precisely defined.

Section 9.2: Causality and Mill's Methods

A. Many instances of reasoning assume a relationship of cause and effect. But the meaning of this relationship is seriously ambiguous. Three alternative meanings of "cause" can be identified, as follows:

1. The cause may mean the sufficient condition for producing the effect. So,

if the cause occurs, then the effect occurs.

2. The cause may mean one of many necessary conditions for the occurrence of the effect. Based on the conditional definition of a necessary condition, if the effect occurs, then the cause occurs.

3. The cause may mean both sufficient and necessary conditions for the occurrence of the effect. So, the cause occurs if and only if the effect occurs.

B. The nineteenth-century philosopher John Stuart Mill defined five methods for identifying causal connections between events. A variation of these methods is presented as follows:

1. The method of agreement consists of the direct method of agreement and the inverse method of agreement.

a. The direct method of agreement

(1) Assume that we can recognize a single factor that is present in a number of different occurrences in which the effect is also present. Of course, we cannot examine all occurrences in which the effect is present.

(2) The direct method consists of the stipulation that this single factor is probably a cause of the effect, based on the conception above that the cause is a necessary condition for the occurrence of the effect.

(3) Of course, we cannot be sure that this particular factor is a necessary condition of the effect, because there are many unexamined cases of the effect which may not include the causal factor that is proposed.

b. The inverse method of agreement

(1) Assume that we can recognize a set of conditions in which the known effect is absent. Find a factor that is absent under this set of conditions.

(2) The inverse method of agreement consists of recognizing some single factor that is absent under the same conditions that the effect is absent.

(3) The presence of this factor may be a causal factor for the occurrence of the known effects, in the sense that the cause is a sufficient condition for producing the effect. Of course, this identification of the causal factor for certain known effects at best establishes an inductive argument of a probable cause.

2. The double method of agreement combines both direct method of agree and inverse method of agreement.

a. For all cases in which a given effect is present, identify a factor that is also present.

b. For all cases in which a given effect is absent, identify a factor that is also absent.

c. This factor, that is present when the effect is present and absent otherwise, may be the cause, in the sense of a necessary and sufficient condition for producing the effect.

3. The method of difference

a. Assume that there are two cases, where one case shows an effect and the other case does not.

b. Identify a factor that is present in the case that shows the effect and also absent in the case that does not show the effect.

c. This factor may be the cause of the effect, in the sense that causation provides the sufficient conditions for producing the effect.

4. The joint method of agreement and different requires that the direct method of agreement be combined with the method of difference. In this case causation assumes the notion of a sufficient and necessary condition.

5. The method of residues consists of separating from a group of causally connected conditions and phenomena those strands of causal connection that are already known, leaving the required causal connection as the "residue".

6. The method of concomitant variation consists of identifying a causal connection between two conditions by matching variations in one conditions with variations in another.

Section 9.3: Probability

A. Consider some examples of probabilities.

1. The probability of selecting a diamond card from a full deck is 1/4.

2. The probability that a 20 year-old man will live to 75 is 0.63.

3. There is a high probability that Margaret and Peter will get married.

B. Three different conceptions of probability can be identified.

1. Classical conception

a. The probability of an event $\underline{A}$ is the ratio of the number of favorable outcomes, $\underline{f}$, to the number of possible outcomes, $\underline{n}$.

b. $P(A) = f/n$.

c. Two assumptions are necessary.

(1) All possible outcomes are considered

(2) All possible outcomes are equally probable.

2. Relative frequency conception

a. The probability of an event A is the ratio of the number of observed favorable outcomes, f_o, to the total number of observed outcomes, n_o.

b. $P(A) = f_o/n_o$.

3. Subjective probability conception

a. Subjective probability refers to the beliefs of individuals.

b. For example, "He bets 7 to 4 that the horse wins the race".

C. Probability Calculus allows us to compute the probabilities of compound events from individual probabilities of events.

1. Maximum probability that an event will occur = 1.

2. Minimum probability that an event will occur = 0.

D. Rules of Probability

1. Restricted conjunction rule

a. Assume that two events are independent of each other, as in the case of tossing a coin. What is the probability that both of these events will occur?

b. The probability that event A and B both occur together = P(A and B) = P(A) x P(B).

c. What is the probability of rolling consecutive "5's" on a fair die? P(F1 & F2) = (1/6) x (1/6) = 1/36.

2. General conjunction rule.

a. Assume that the occurrence of one event alters the chances for the occurrence of another event. This assumption conveys the property of dependence.

b. Use formula: P(A and B) = P(A) x P(B given A).

c. The selection of one 'jack' alters the chances of selecting a second jack. Use formula: P(J1 & J2) = P(J1) x P(J2 given J1)

d. For example, assume a container has 10 red balls, 6 green balls, and 9 yellow balls. What is the probability of drawing green as the first ball and yellow as the secondball? P(G and Y) = 6/25 x 9/24.

e. The general conjunction rule includes the restricted conjunction rule. When two event are independent of each other, as in cases of the restricted rule, the P(B) = P(B given A)

3. Restricted Disjunction rule

a. Assume that two events are mutually exclusive, because they cannot both occur. Also, assume that these two events are independent of each other.

b. The probability of selecting either event is the summation of the probabilities of both events.

c. For example, what is the probability of selecting either a king or an ace in a single blank draw of a card? P(K or A) = P(K) + P(A). 4/52 + 4/52 = 2/13.

c. These two event cannot both happen together.

4. General Disjunction Rule

a. This rule is used to compute the probability of either of two events, whether or not they are mutually exclusive. This means that the events might both occur together, in which case they are not mutually exclusive.

b. However, the events are still independent of each other, since the occurrence of one event does not change the probability of the occurrence of the other event.

c. Rule P(A or B) = P(A) + P(B) - [P(A) x P(B)]

d. What is the probability of getting at least one six when rolling a pair of dice?

P(S1 or S2) = P(S1) + P(S2) - P(S1 and S2)

= 1/6 + 1/6 - (1/6 x 1/6) =

2/6 - 1/36 = 11/36.

5. Negation Rule.

a. What is the probability that event X will not happen, assuming we know the probability that X will happen?

b. If P(X) = n, then P(not-X) = 1-n.

c. What is the probability of not drawing an ace from one draw of standard deck?

d. P(not A) = 1 - 4/52 = 48/52 = 12/13.

6. Using the negation rule.

a. First compute the probability of getting no sixes:

P(no sixes) = 5/6 x 5/6 x 5/6 = 125/216.

b. Then use the negation rule:

P(at least one six) = 1 - P(no sixes) =

1 - 125/216 = 91/216.

Section 9.4: Statistical Reasoning

A. A common form of statistic evidence is gathered from analyzing a sample, which is any member, or group of members, of a population.

1. The purpose of sampling is to make an inference about some characteristics of the population based on characteristics of the sample. Such an inference is typically inductive.

2. Many uses of sampling evidence rest on the following claim: the percentage of the sample with a particular characteristic in relation to the whole population is the same as the percentage of the population with the same characteristic.

3. The success of such an argument requires that the sample is representative (unbiased) in relation to the population as a whole.

B. Statistical evidence is also presented by measurement of averages. The notion of average has three different meanings: the mean, the median, and the mode.

1. The mean value of a set of measurements = df. the sum of the set of measurements divided by the number of measurements in the set.

2. The median of a set of measurements = df. the middle measurement value when the measurements are arranged in order of magnitude. In such a case, there is an equal number of measurement values above the middle value as there are below the middle value.

3. The mode = df. the particular data value that occurs with the greatest

frequency.

C. A graph is a common device for displaying a set of measurements, so that each measurement is assigned a particular category.

1. A pictogram is a diagram that compares two situations through drawings that differ either in size or in the number of entities depicted.

2. Graphs and pictograms are highly convenient and informative ways to represent statistical data, but they are also susceptible to misuses and misinterpretation.

D. A percentage is a type of ratio multiplied by 100.

1. The numerator of this ratio is the number of members of the population with a certain property, and the denominator is the total number of members in the whole population.

2. One form of misleading evidence occurs when a comparison of percentages from different populations is implied, but the base percentage figure is omitted.

Section 9.5: Hypothetical Reasoning

A. Hypothetical reasoning is needed when scientists engage in experimental testing, for the purpose of evaluating the probable truth or the falsity of an hypothesis. But the precise formulation of hypothetical reasoning is controversial.

B. The basic components of every instance of hypothetical reasoning are as follows:

1. The hypothesis is a statement under evaluation, whose truth or falsity is unknown prior to the performance of the experiment.

2. The initial conditions are statements describing the known events in such a

way that the hypothesis is applied to such events. Within a scientific experiment, initial conditions specify the context of application for a particular hypothesis.

3. The prediction is a statement describing the possible occurrence of an event at a particular time and place, under the assumption that the hypothesis and initial conditions are true. In each prediction, the hypothesis is not actually known to be true, but it is tentatively assumed to be true as a conjecture.

C. According to the method of hypothetical reasoning, the prediction is logically deducible from the conjunction of the hypothesis and initial conditions.

1. In an argument form, the conclusion expresses the prediction and the premises convey the hypothesis and initial conditions.

2. Based on this argument form, if the prediction is false, then the conjunction of hypothesis and initial conditions is false. Moreover, the initial conditions are assumed to be true in this case. It follows in this case that the hypothesis is false.

3. Based on this argument form, if the prediction is true, then this argument may provide additional inductive support for the truth of the conjunction of the hypothesis and initial conditions.

4. But no finite number of true predictions can ever lead to the deductive justification of the hypothesis and initial conditions.

Exercise Answers to Select Problems

Exercise 1.1

Part I

2. P: The good, according to Plato, is that which furthers a person's real interests.
   C: In any given case when the good is known, men will seek it.

5. P_1: Artists and poets look at the world and seek relationships and order.
   P_2: But they translate their ideas to canvas, or to marble, or into poetic images.
   P_3: Scientists try to find relationships between different objects and events.
   P_4: To express the order they find, they create hypotheses and theories.
   C: The great scientific theories are easily compared to great art and great literature.

8. P: Like a frame or the wake of a boat, the form of a plant changes slowly but the components are in continual flux.
   C: The motion of the components can be analyzed in terms of fluid flow.

11. P: The drive for profits underlies the very existence of business organizations.
    C: A most important function of an accounting system is to provide information about the profitability of a business.

14. P_1: The average working man can support no more than two children.
    P_2: The average working woman can take care of no more than two children in decent fashion.
    C: Women of the working class, especially wage workers, should not have more than two children at most.

17. P_1: Corn is an annual crop.
    P_2: Butchers meat is a crop which requires four or five years to grow.
    P_3: An acre of land will produce a much smaller quantity of the one species of food (meat) than the other.
    C: The inferiority of the quantity (of meat) must be compensated by the superiority of the price.

20. P_1: It is generally accepted that by constantly swimming with its mouth open, the shark is simply avoiding suffocation.
    P_2: This assures a continuous flow of oxygen-laden water into their mouths, over their gills, and out through the gill slits.
    C: Contrary to the tales of some scuba divers, the toothsome, gaping grin on the mouth of an approaching shark is not necessarily anticipatory.

23. P_1: The secondary light [from the moon] does not inherently belong to the moon, and is not received from any star or from the sun.
P_2: In the whole universe there is no other body left but the earth.
C: The lunar body (or any other dark and sunless orb) is illuminated by the earth.

Exercise 1.1
Part II

2. The creation of a multilingual society is contrary to the best interests of all of us.
5. The sale and purchase of recreational drugs should be legalized.
8. Animal lovers should act to prevent dog-sled races.

Exercise 1.1
Part III

2. Argument: A group of statements one or more of which (the premises) are claimed to provide support for, or reasons to believe, one of the others (the conclusion).
5. Conclusion: The statement in an argument that the premises are claimed to support or imply.
8. Inference: The reasoning process used to produce an argument.
11. Truth value: The attribute by which a statement is either true or false.

Exercise 1.1
Part IV

2. False.
5. True.
8. True.

Exercise 1.2
Part I

2. Nonargument; conditional statement.
5. Nonargument; lacks an inferential claim (piece of advice).
8. Argument (conclusion: Fiction provides us with the opportunity to ponder how people react in uncommon situations, and to deduce moral lessons, psychological principles, and philosophical insights from their behavior).
11. Argument (conclusion: When the insurer unreasonably and in bad faith withholds payment of the claim of its insured, it is subject to liability in tort).

Exercise 1.2
Part I continued

14. Nonargument; lacks an inferential claim (report of an argument).
17. Nonargument; lacks an inferential claim (expository passage or statement of opinion).
20. Nonargument; lacks an inferential claim (temporal meaning of "since").
23. Argument (conclusion: The coarsest type of humor is the practical joke).
26. Argument (conclusion: Words are slippery customers).
29. Nonargument; lacks an inferential claim (opinion).
32. Both an argument and an explanation (conclusion: Men are less likely to develop osteoporosis until later in life than women and seldom suffer as severely).
35. Argument (conclusion: The plane mirror remains an important element in the modern arsenal of sophisticated optical devices).

Exercise 1.2
Part II

2. Argument (conclusion: Meat eating is not only hypocritical, it is immoral).
5. Argument (conclusion: In opposing obligatory prayer in the public schools I am actually serving God).
8. Argument (conclusion: While women make 99 percent of male starting salaries in entry-level positions, when they are ten years into their careers they are making 91 percent of what men with identical backgrounds and training earn).

Exercise 1.2
Part III

2. Antecedent: The component of a conditional statement that immediately follows the word "if", the component of a conditional statement that is not the consequent.
5. Necessary condition: The condition represented by the consequent of a conditional statement.
8. Explanans: The component of an explanation that explains the event indicated by the explanandum.

Exercise 1.2
Part IV

2. False.
5. True.
8. True.
11. False.
14. True.

Exercise 1.3
Part I

2. Inductive (argument based on signs).
5. Inductive (generalization).
8. Deductive (the conclusion follows necessarily from the premises).
11. Deductive (argument from definition).
14. Deductive (hypothetical syllogism; also, the conclusion follows necessarily from the premises).
17. Deductive (the conclusion follows necessarily from the premises).
20. Deductive (the conclusion follows necessarily from the premise).
23. Inductive (prediction; also, the conclusion follows only probably from the premises).
26. Deductive (the conclusion follows necessarily from the premises).
29. Inductive (causal inference; also, the tentative flavor of "should indicate" suggests an inductive argument).

Exercise 1.3
Part II

2. Inductive argument: An argument in which the premises are claimed to provide only probable support for the conclusion.
5. Argument based on mathematics: A deductive argument in which the conclusion depends on some purely arithmetic or geometric computation or measurement.
8. Hypothetical syllogism: A syllogism having a conditional statement for one or both of its premises.
11. Argument from authority: An inductive argument in which the conclusion rests upon a statement made by some presumed authority or witness.
14. Particular statement: A statement that makes a claim about one or more (but not all) members of a class.

Exercise 1.3
Part III

2. True.
5. False.
8. False.
11. True.
14. False.

Exercise 1.4
Part I

2. Invalid (true premises, false conclusion), unsound.
5. valid (true premises, true conclusion), sound.
8. Assuming the missing premise is "All hexagons have six sides" the argument is invalid, (false premise, false conclusion), unsound.

Exercise 1.4
Part II

2. Strong (true premise, probably true conclusion), cogent.
5. Weak (false premise, probably true conclusion), uncogent.
8. Strong (false premise, probably true conclusion), uncogent.

Exercise 1.4
Part III

2. Inductive, weak.
5. Deductive, valid.
8. Deductive, invalid.
11. Inductive, weak.
14. Deductive, valid, unsound.
17. Deductive, valid.
20. Deductive, invalid.

Exercise 1.4
Part IV

2. Invalid argument: A deductive argument in which the premises do not provide necessary support for the conclusion.
5. Strong argument: An inductive argument in which the premises provide probably support for the conclusion.
8. Uncogent argument: An inductive argument that is either weak or has one or more false premises (or both).

Exercise 1.4
Part V

2. True.
5. True.
8. False.
11. False.
14. False.

Exercise 1.5
Part I

2.	No C are E.	No cats are dogs.	(T)
	Some P are not C.	Some animals are not cats.	(T)
	Some E are not P.	Some dogs are not animals.	(F)
5.	Some P are W.	Some animals are dogs.	(T)
	No W are T.	No dogs are fish.	(T)
	No P are T.	No animals are fish.	(F)
8.	Some T are S.	Some cats are animals.	(T)
	Some S are U.	Some animals are dogs.	(T)
	Some T are U.	Some cats are dogs.	(F)

Exercise 1.5
Part II

2.	If C then P.	If George Washington was assassinated, then George Washington is dead.
	P	George Washington is dead.
	C	George Washington was assassinated.
5.	All H who are P are D.	All humans who are female are women.
	All H are D.	All humans are women.
8.	All M that are R are B that are I.	All animals that are cats are felines that are mammals.
	All M are I.	All animals are mammals.

Exercise 1.6
Part I

2. 

5. 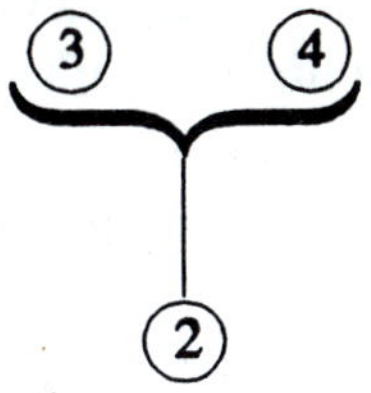

8. 

Exercise 4.1

2. Quantifier: some; Subject term: college students; Copula: are; Predicate term: avid devotees of soap operas.
5. Quantifier: all; Subject term: trials in which a coerced confession is read to the jury; Copula: are; Predicate term: trials in which a guilty verdict can be reversed.
8. Quantifier: some; Subject term: universities that emphasize research; Copula: are not; Predicate term: institutions that neglect undergraduate education.

Exercise 4.2
Part I

2. **A** proposition, universal affirmative, subject distributed, predicate undistributed.
5. **A** proposition, universal affirmative, subject distributed, predicate undistributed.
8. **O** proposition, particular negative, subject undistributed, predicate distributed.

Exercise 4.3
Part II

2. valid.
5. Invalid.
8. valid.

Exercise 4.4
Part I

2.	Some non-B are non-A.	Und.
5.	Some B are not non-A.	Und.
8.	Obversion	True
11.	Contraposition	True

Exercise 4.4
Part II

2a. No radically egalitarian societies are societies that preserve individual liberties. (Logically equivalent).

b. All cult leaders are people who brainwash their followers. (Logically equivalent).

c. Some college football coaches are not persons who slip money to their players. (Logically equivalent).

d. Some budgetary cutbacks are actions unfair to the poor. (Logically equivalent).

Exercise 4.4
Part III

2. valid.
5. valid.
8. Invalid (illicit conversion).

Exercise 4.5
Part I

2. (a) undetermined, (b) undetermined, (c) true.
5. (a) undetermined, (b) false, (c) undetermined.
8. (a) true, (b) false, (c) true.

Exercise 4.5
Part II

2. Invalid (illicit subalternation).
5. valid.
8. Invalid (illicit subcontrary).

Exercise 4.5
Part III

2. All A are non-B. (False).
5. Some A are non-B. (Undetermined).
8. Some A are B. (False).
11. Contradictory (False)
14. Subalternation (Undetermined)
17. Contraposition (True)
20. Subcontrary (True)

Exercise 4.5
Part IV

2. No non-G are E.
   Some non-G are not E. (Subalt.)
   Some non-E are not G. (Contrap.)

5. No non-P are F.
   No F are non-P. (Conv.)
   All F are P. (Obv).
   F: Some F are not P. (Contradic.)

8. F: No non-H are F.
   F: No F are non-H. (Obv.)
   F: All F are H. (Conv.)
   Some F are not H. (Contradic.)

Exercise 4.6
Part I

2. No women miliary officers are persons eligible for combat duty.
5. Some guilt feelings are not psychological aberrations.
8. All television shows that depict violence are shows that incite violence.
11. All times warmth is applied to pain are times warmth relieves pain.
14. All vehicles suitable for deep space exploration are nuclear powered vehicles.
17. All pregnant women who drink alcohol are women who risk giving birth to a deformed child.
20. All things identical to the electroscope are devices for detecting static electricity.
23. No times in January are times the Kentucky Derby is run.

26. All times eclipses occur are times the moon is full.
29. No rats are animals that left the sinking ship, and all non-rats are animals that left the sinking ship.
32. All persons who hesitate are persons who are lost.
35. All persons who suffer allergic reactions are persons with a weakened immune system.
38. All monkeys are mammals.

Exercise 4.6
Part II

2. All cars that yuppies drive are BMWs.
5. All substances identical to cobalt are ferromagnetic metals.
8. All companies identical to IBM are companies facing restructuring in the years ahead.

Exercise 6.1
Part I

2. $G \cdot \sim P$
5. $L \supset B$
8. $L \supset B$
11. $H \supset (T \cdot F)$
14. $\sim(W \cdot H)$
17. $\sim(C \vee H)$
20. $(J \supset V) \supset T$
23. $\sim C \vee (R \supset B)$
26. $J \cdot (T \vee C)$
29. $(P \supset T) \cdot \sim G$
32. $W \supset [G \supset (E \cdot K)]$
35. $A \equiv J$
38. $M \supset (A \supset Q)$

Exercise 6.1
Part II

2. Not WFF
5. Not WFF
8. Not WFF

Exercise 6.2
Part I

2. Horseshoe
5. Wedge
8. Triple bar

Exercise 6.2
Part II

2.	$N \cdot L$	True
5.	$E \vee C$	True
8.	$L \equiv C$	False
11.	$(L \cdot E) \vee (N \cdot \sim E)$	True
14.	$\sim C \vee (N \cdot E)$	False

Exercise 6.2
Part III

2. True
5. True
8. False
11. True
14. True
17. True
20. False
23. True

Exercise 6.2
Part IV

2. Undetermined
5. True
8. False
11. False
14. True

Exercise 6.3
Part I

2. Continent
5. Self-contradictory
8. Contingent
11. Self-contradictory
14. Tautologous

Exercise 6.3
Part II

2. Neither
5. Logically equivalent
8. Logically equivalent

Exercise 6.3
Part III

2. The British will not leave Northern Ireland and Ireland will be unified. (Construct a truth table for Bradshaw's statement and examine the one lone on which it turns out true.)
5. Martinez's statement is tautologous; therefore, she has told us nothing about a tax reduction.
8. Leftie pried open the window, Hank did not enter the building, but Pinkie did enter. (Construct a truth table for each statement and examine the one line on which Stephen's statement and the negation of Michael's statement are both true. This should be the third line.)

Exercise 6.4
Part I

2. $\underline{B}$
   $B \vee A$ (Valid)

5. $R \supset \sim C$
   $\underline{W \supset \sim C}$
   $R \supset W$ (Invalid)

8. $C \supset H$
   $\underline{\sim H \cdot C}$
   N (valid)

Exercise 6.4
Part II

2. Invalid
5. Invalid
8. Invalid
11. Invalid
14. valid
17. valid

Exercise 6.5

2. Invalid
5. valid
8. Invalid
11. valid
14. Invalid

Exercise 6.6
Part I

2. HS
5. MP
8. AC
11. Invalid
14. Invalid
17. MT
20. DA

Exercise 6.6
Part II

2. $J \supset \sim I$
   $\underline{\sim I}$
   J (AC)

5. $T \vee \sim D$
   $\underline{T}$
   D (Inv.)

8. $G \supset E$
   $\underline{\sim G}$
   $\sim E$ (DA)

11. $P \supset W$
    $\underline{\sim P}$
    $\sim W$ (DA)

14. $I \vee A$
    $\underline{I}$
    $\sim A$ (Inv.)

17. $\sim C \vee \sim A$
    $\underline{A}$
    $\sim C$ (DS)

Exercise 6.6
Part II continued

20. $(T \supset G) \cdot (\sim T \supset P)$
$\underline{T \vee \sim T}$
$G \vee P$ (CD)

Exercise 6.6
Part III

2. $(V \supset F) \cdot (H \supset L)$
$\underline{V \vee H}$
$F \vee L$ (CD)

Here it is easy to escape between the horns. If we build our home half way up the hillside, then it will neither be in the valley or on the hilltop, thus falsifying the disjunctive premise. It is also easy to grasp the dilemma by the horns: Build on the hilltop, but install lightening arresters. Here is a counterdilemma:

If we build our home in the valley, then it will not be hit by lightning; and, if we build it on the hilltop, then it will not be struck by floods. We must either build in the valley or on the hilltop. Therefore, either our home will not be hit by lightning or not be struck by floods.

5. $(P \supset M) \cdot (\sim P \supset S)$
$\underline{P \vee \sim P}$
$M \vee S$ (CD)

It is impossible to escape between the horns. One could grasp the dilemma by the horns by arguing that physicians should avail the terminally ill patient of the opportunity to pull the plug on himself. If the patient is in a coma, a living will could avoid the dilemma.

8. $(A \supset F) \cdot (\sim A \supset L)$
$\underline{A \vee \sim A}$
$F \vee L$ (CD)

Since the second premise is tautology, one cannot escape between the horns. One could grasp the dilemma by the horns by attacking the left hand horn: It the merchant can prove that detaining a suspected shop-lifter is reasonable under the circumstances, and if the merchant confines the search to the shopper's parcels, the merchant can accomplish his/her purpose and void charges of false arrest. A counterdilemma:

If merchants arrest suspected shop-lifters, they will avoid loss of merchandise; if they don't arrest them, they will avoid charges of false imprisonment. Merchants must either arrest or not arrest suspected shop-lifters. Therefore, they will either avoid loss of merchandise or avoid charges of false imprisonment.

Exercise 6.6
Part IV

2. If we remain on standard time, then the grass will get one hour less sunlight. *If the grass gets one hour less sunlight, then it will stay greener. Therefore, if we remain on standard time, then the grass will stay greener. (HS)

5. If voluntary school prayer makes our children more moral, then mandatory church attendance on Sunday will do wonders for the rest of us. Mandatory church attendance on Sunday will not do wonders for the rest of us. Therefore, voluntary school prayer does not make our children more moral. (MT)

8. If the death penalty deters at least one person from becoming a murderer, then it is justified. The death penalty does deter at least one person from becoming a murderer. Therefore, the death penalty is justified. (MP)

   If the families and friend of innocent victims have the right to see effective retribution, then the death penalty is justified. The families and friends of innocent victims do have the right to see effective retribution. Therefore, the death penalty is justified. (MP)

   If terminating the life of a killer is more economical than keeping him in jail at the taxpayer's expense, then the death penalty is justified. Terminating the life of a killer is more economical than keeping him in jail at the taxpayer's expense. Therefore, the death penalty is justified. (MP)

   If everyone will have greater respect for the judicial system if the death penalty is imposed, then the death penalty is justified. Everyone will have greater respect for the judicial system if the death penalty is imposed. Therefore, the death penalty is justified. (MP)

Exercise 7.1
Part I

(2)

1.	$\sim(S \equiv T) \supset (\sim P \supset Q)$	
2.	$(S \equiv T) \supset P$	
3.	$\sim P$	/ Q
4.	$\sim(S \equiv T)$	2, 3, MT
5.	$\sim P \supset Q$	1, 4, MP
6.	Q	3, 5, MP

(5)

1.	$H \supset [\sim E \supset (C \supset \sim D)]$	
2.	$\sim D \supset E$	
3.	$E \vee H$	
4.	$\sim E$	/ $\sim C$
5.	H	3, 4, DS
6.	$\sim E \supset (C \supset \sim D)$	1, 5, MP
7.	$C \supset \sim D$	4, 6, MP
8.	$C \supset E$	2, 7, HS
9.	$\sim C$	4, 8, MT

Exercise 7.1
Part II

(2)

1.	$(K \cdot O) \supset (N \vee T)$	
2.	$K \cdot O$	/ $N \vee T$
3.	$N \vee T$	1, 2, MP

(5)

1.	$\sim C \supset (A \supset C)$	
2.	$\sim C$	/ $\sim A$
3.	$A \supset C$	1, 2, MP
4.	$\sim A$	2, 3, MT

(8)

1.	$P \supset (G \supset T)$	
2.	$Q \supset (T \supset E)$	
3.	P	
4.	Q	/ $G \supset E$
5.	$G \supset T$	1, 3, MP
6.	$T \supset E$	2, 4, MP
7.	$G \supset E$	5, 6, HS

Exercise 7.1
Part II continued

(11)

1.	$A \supset (E \supset \sim F)$	
2.	$H \vee (\sim F \supset M)$	
3.	A	
4.	$\sim H$	/ $E \supset M$
5.	$E \supset \sim F$	1, 3, MP
6.	$\sim F \supset M$	2, 4, DS
7.	$E \supset M$	5, 6, HS

(14)

1.	$\sim M \vee (B \vee \sim T)$	
2.	$B \supset W$	
3.	$\sim \sim M$	
4.	$\sim W$	/ $\sim T$
5.	$B \vee \sim T$	1, 3, DS
6.	$\sim B$	2, 4, MT
7.	$\sim T$	5, 6, DS

(17)

1.	$(B \supset \sim M \supset (T \supset \sim S)$	
2.	$B \supset K$	
3.	$K \supset \sim M$	
4.	$\sim S \supset N$	/ $T \supset N$
5.	$B \supset \sim M$	2, 3, HS
6.	$T \supset \sim S$	1, 5, MP
7.	$T \supset N$	4, 6, HS

(20)

1.	$\sim N \supset [(B \supset D) \supset (N \vee \sim E)]$	
2.	$(B \supset E)$ U $\sim N$	
3.	$B \supset D$	
4.	$D \supset E$	/ $\sim D$
5.	$B \supset E$	3, 4, HS
6.	$\sim N$	2, 5, MP
7.	$(B \supset D) \supset (N \vee \sim E)$	1, 6, MP
8.	$N \vee \sim E$	3, 7, MP
9.	$\sim E$	6, 8, DS
10.	$\sim D$	4, 9, MT

Exercise 7.1
Part III

(2)	1. $E \supset O$		
	2. $R \vee \sim O$		
	3. $\sim R$	/ $\sim E$	
	4. $\sim O$	2, 3, DS	
	5. $\sim E$	1, 4, MT	

(5)	1. $C \vee (H \supset R)$	
	2. $S \vee (R \supset E)$	
	3. $\sim C$	
	4. $\sim S$	/ $H \supset E$
	5. $H \supset R$	1, 3, DS
	6. $R \supset E$	2, 4, DS
	7. $H \supset E$	5, 6, HS

(8)	1. $R \vee B$	
	2. $(I \supset H) \supset \sim R$	
	3. $L \supset (I \supset T)$	
	4. $T \supset H$	
	5. L	/ B
	6. $I \supset T$	3, 5, MP
	7. $I \supset H$	4, 6, HS
	8. $\sim R$	2, 7, MP
	9. B	1, 8, DS

Exercise 7.2
Part I

(2)	1. $(P \vee S) \supset (E \supset F)$	
	2. $(P \vee T) \supset (G \supset H)$	
	3. $(P \vee U) \supset (E \vee G)$	
	4. P	/$F \vee H$
	5. $P \vee S$	4, Add
	6. $E \supset S$	1, 5, MP
	7. $P \vee T$	4, Add
	8. $G \supset H$	2, 7, MP
	9. $P \vee U$	4, Add
	10. $E \vee G$	3, 9, MP
	11. $(E \supset F) \cdot (G \supset H)$	6, 8, Conj
	12. $F \vee H$	10, 11, CD

Exercise 7.2
Part I continued

(5)	1. (R ⊃ H) · (S ⊃ I)	
	2. (~H · ~L) ⊃ (R ∨ S)	
	3. ~H · (K ⊃ T)	
	4. H ∨ ~L	/ I ∨ M
	5. ~H	3, Simp
	6. ~L	4, 5, DS
	7. ~H · ~L	5, 6, Conj
	8. R ∨ S	2, 7, MP
	9. H ∨ I	1, 8, CD
	10. I	5, 9, DS
	11. I ∨ M	10, Add

Exercise 7.2
Part II

(2)	1. E ⊃ (A · C)	
	2. A ⊃ (F · E)	
	3. E	/ F
	4. A · C	1, 3, MP
	5. A	4, Simp
	6. F · E	2, 5, MP
	7. F	6, Simp

(5)	1. (~F ∨ X) ⊃ (P ∨ T)	
	2. F ⊃ P	
	3. ~P	/ T
	4. ~F	2, 3, MT
	5. ~F ∨ X	4, Add
	6. P ∨ T	1, 5, MP
	7. T	3, 6, DS

(8)	1. (D ∨ E) ⊃ (G · H)	
	2. G ⊃ ~D	
	3. D · F	/ M
	4. D	3, Simp
	5. D ∨ E	4, Add
	6. G · H	1, 5, MP
	7. G	6, Simp
	8. ~D	2, 7, MP
	9. D ∨ M	4, Add
	10. M	8, 9, DS

Exercise 7.2
Part II

(11)	1. (C ⊃ N) · E	
	2. D ∨ (N ⊃ D)	
	3. ~D	/ ~C ∨ P
	4. N ⊃ D	2, 3, DS
	5. ~N	3, 4, MT
	6. C ⊃ N	1, Simp
	7. ~C	5, 6, MT
	8. ~C ∨ P	7, Add

(14)	1. (U · ~~P) ⊃ Q	
	2. ~O ⊃ U	
	3. ~P ⊃ O	
	4. ~O · T	/ Q
	5. ~O	4, Simp
	6. U	2, 5, MP
	7. ~~P	3, 5, MT
	8. U · ~~P	6, 7, Conj
	9. Q	1, 8, MP

(17)	1. (~K · ~N) ⊃ [(~P ⊃ K) · (~R ⊃ G)]	
	2. K ⊃ N	
	3. ~N · B	
	4. ~P ∨ ~R	/G
	5. ~N	3, Simp
	6. ~K	2, 5, MT
	7. ~K · ~N	5, 6, Conj
	8. (~P ⊃ K) · (~R ⊃ G)	1, 7, MP
	9. K ∨ G	4, 8, CD
	10. G	6, 9, DS

Exercise 7.2
Part II continued

(20) 1. $(W \cdot X) \supset (Q \vee R)$
2. $(S \vee F) \supset (Q \vee W)$
3. $(S \vee G) \supset (\sim Q \supset X)$
4. $Q \vee S$
5. $\sim Q \cdot H$ / R
6. $\sim Q$ 5, Simp
7. S 4, 6, DS
8. $S \vee F$ 7, Add
9. $Q \vee W$ 2, 8, MP
10. W 6, 9, DS
11. $S \vee G$ 7, Add
12. $\sim Q \supset X$ 3, 11, MP
13. X 6, 12, MP
14. $W \cdot X$ 10, 13, Conj
15. $Q \vee R$ 1, 14, MP
16. R 6, 15, DS

Exercise 7.2
Part III

(2) 1. $(C \cdot \sim E) \supset (E \vee T)$
2. $T \cdot C$ / $Q \vee O$
3. T 2, Simp
4. $Q \cdot F$ 1, 3, MP
5. Q 4, Simp
6. $Q \vee O$ 5, Add

(5) 1. $H \supset [(I \vee P) \supset E]$
2. $(H \vee W) \supset \sim E$
3. H / $\sim(I \vee P)$
4. $H \vee W$ 3, Add
5. $\sim E$ 2, 4, MP
6. $(I \vee P) \supset E$ 1, 3, MP
7. $\sim(I \vee P)$ 5, 6, MT

Exercise 7.2
Part III continued

(8)	1. (F ∨ A) ⊃ (H · P)	
	2. L ⊃ A	
	3. D ⊃ F	
	4. (D ∨ L) · I	/ H
	5. (D ⊃ F) · (L ⊃ A)	2, 3, Conj
	6. D ∨ L	4, Simp
	7. F ∨ A	5, 6, CD
	8. H · P	1, 7, MP
	9. H	8, Simp

Exercise 7.3
Part I

(2)	1. (K · P) ∨ (K · Q)	
	2. P ⊃ ~K	/ Q ∨ T
	3. K · (P ∨ Q)	1, Dist
	4. K	3, Simp
	5. ~ ~K	4, DN
	6. ~P	2, 5, MT
	7. (P ∨ Q) · K	3, Com
	8. P ∨ Q	7, Simp
	9. Q	6, 8, DS
	10. Q ∨ T	9, Add

(5)	1. A · (F · L)	
	2. A ⊃ (U ∨ W)	
	3. F ⊃ (U ∨ X)	/ U ∨ (W · X)
	4. (A · F) · L	1, Assoc
	5. A · F	4, Simp
	6. A	5, Simp
	7. U ∨ W	2, 6, MP
	8. F · A	5, Con
	9. F	8, Simp
	10. U ∨ X	3, 9, MP
	11. (U ∨ W) · (U ∨ X)	7, 10, Conj
	12. U ∨ (W · X)	11, Dist

Exercise 7.3
Part II

(2)

1.	$J \vee (K \cdot L)$	
2.	$\sim K$	/ J
3.	$(J \vee K) \cdot (J \vee L)$	1, Dist
4.	$J \vee K$	3, Simp
5.	$K \vee J$	4, Com
6.	J	2, 5, DS

(5)

1.	$Q \vee (L \vee C)$	
2.	$\sim C$	/ $L \vee Q$
3.	$(Q \vee L) \vee C$	1, Assoc
4.	$C \vee (Q \vee L)$	3, Com
5.	$Q \vee L$	2, 4, DS
6.	$L \vee Q$	5, Com

(8)

1.	$(E \cdot I) \vee (M \cdot U)$	
2.	$\sim E$	/ M
3.	$\sim E \vee \sim I$	2, Add
4.	$\sim (E \cdot I)$	3, DM
5.	$M \cdot U$	1, 4, DS
6.	M	5, Simp

(11)

1.	$(D \cdot S) \vee (C \cdot T)$	
2.	$\sim T$	/ S
3.	$\sim T \vee \sim C$	2, Add
4.	$\sim C \vee \sim T$	3, Com
5.	$\sim (C \cdot T)$	4, DM
6.	$(C \cdot T) \vee (D \cdot S)$	1, Com
7.	$D \cdot S$	5, 6, DS
8.	$S \cdot D$	7, Com
9.	S	8, Simp

(14)

1.	$[(I \vee M) \vee G] \supset \sim G$	
2.	$M \vee G$	/ M
3.	$(M \vee G) \vee I$	2, Add
4.	$I \vee (M \vee G)$	3, Com
5.	$(I \vee M) \vee G$	4, Assoc
6.	$\sim G$	1, 5, MP
7.	$G \vee M$	2, Com
8.	M	6, 7, DS

Exercise 7.3
Part II continued

(17)

1.	$S \vee (I \cdot \sim J)$	
2.	$S \supset \sim R$	
3.	$\sim J \supset \sim Q$	/ $\sim(R \cdot Q)$
4.	$(S \vee I) \cdot (S \vee \sim J)$	1, Dist
5.	$(S \vee \sim J) \cdot (S \vee I)$	4, Com
6.	$S \vee \sim J$	5, Simp
7.	$(S \supset \sim R) \cdot (\sim J \supset \sim Q)$	2, 3, Conj
8.	$\sim R \vee \sim Q$	6, 7, CD
9.	$\sim(R \cdot Q)$	8, DM

(20)

1.	$(\sim M \vee E) \supset (S \supset U)$	
2.	$(\sim Q \vee E) \supset (U \supset H)$	
3.	$(\sim(M \vee Q)$	/ $S \supset H$
4.	$\sim M \cdot \sim Q$	3, DM
5.	$\sim M$	4, Simp
6.	$\sim M \vee E$	5, Add
7.	$S \supset U$	1, 6, MP
8.	$\sim Q \cdot \sim M$	4, Com
9.	$\sim Q$	8, Simp
10.	$\sim Q \vee E$	9, Add
11.	$U \supset H$	2, 10, MP
12.	$S \supset H$	7, 11, HS

(23)

1.	$\sim(A \cdot G)$	
2.	$\sim(A \cdot E)$	
3.	$G \vee E$	/ $\sim(A \cdot F)$
4.	$\sim A \vee \sim G$	1, DM
5.	$\sim A \vee \sim E$	2, DM
6.	$(\sim A \vee \sim G) \cdot (\sim A \vee \sim E)$	4, 5, Conj
7.	$\sim A \vee (\sim G \cdot \sim E)$	6, Dist
8.	$\sim A \vee \sim(G \vee E)$	7, DM
9.	$\sim(G \vee E) \vee \sim A$	8, Com
10.	$\sim\sim(G \vee E)$	3, DN
11.	$\sim A$	9, 10, DS
12.	$\sim A \vee \sim F$	11, Add
13.	$\sim(A \cdot F)$	12, DM

Exercise 7.3
Part III

(2)	1. (C · I) ∨ (H · I)	
	2. B ⊃ ~I	/ ~B
	3. (I · C) ∨ (I · H)	1, Com
	4. I · (C ∨ H)	3, Dist
	5. I	4, Simp
	6. ~ ~I	5, DN
	7. ~B	2, 6, MT

(5)	1. E · (P · B)	
	2. (E · B) ⊃ ~(P · ~M)	/ E · M
	3. E · (B · P)	1, Com
	4. (E · B) · P	3, Assoc
	5. E · B	4, Simp
	6. ~(P · ~M)	2, 5, MP
	7. ~P ∨ ~ ~M	6, DM
	8. P · (E · B)	4, Com
	9. P	8, Simp
	10. ~ ~P	7, 10, DS
	11. ~ ~M	11, DN
	12. M	3, Simp
	13. E	3, Simp
	14. E · M	12, 13, Conj

(8)	1. (L ∨ A) ⊃ ~W	
	2. (N ∨ C) ⊃ ~P	
	3. ~(~W ∨ ~P)	/ ~(A ∨ C)
	4. ~ ~W · ~ ~P	3, DM
	5. ~ ~W	4, Simp
	6. ~(L ∨ A)	1, 5, MT
	7. ~L · ~A	6, DM
	8. ~A · ~L	7, Com
	9. ~A	8, Simp
	10. ~ ~P	4, Com, Simp
	11. ~(N ∨ C)	2, 10, MT
	12. ~N · ~C	11, DM
	13. ~C · ~N	12, Com
	14. ~C	13, Simp
	15. ~A · ~C	9, 14, Conj
	16. ~(A ∨ C)	15, DM

Exercise 7.4
Part I

(2)	1. $C \supset (\sim L \supset Q)$	
	2. $L \supset \sim C$	
	3. $\sim Q$	/ $\sim C$
	4. $(C \cdot \sim L) \supset Q$	1, Exp
	5. $\sim(C \cdot \sim L)$	3, 4, MT
	6. $\sim C \vee \sim\sim L$	5, DM
	7. $\sim C \vee L$	6, DN
	8. $C \supset L$	7, Impl
	9. $C \supset \sim C$	2, 8, HS
	10. $\sim C \vee \sim C$	9, Impl
	11. $\sim C$	10, Taut

(5)	1. $T \supset (H \cdot J)$	
	2. $(H \vee N) \supset T$	/ $T \equiv H$
	3. $\sim T \vee (H \cdot J)$	1, Impl
	4. $(\sim T \vee H) \cdot (\sim T \vee J)$	3, Dist
	5. $\sim T \vee H$	4, Simp
	6. $T \supset H$	5, Impl
	7. $\sim(H \vee N) \vee T$	2, Impl
	8. $(\sim H \cdot \sim N) \vee T$	7, DM
	9. $T \vee (\sim H \cdot \sim N)$	8, Com
	10. $(T \vee \sim H) \cdot (T \vee \sim N)$	9, Dist
	11. $(\sim H \vee T) \cdot (T \vee \sim N)$	10, Com
	12. $\sim H \vee T$	11, Simp
	13. $H \supset T$	12, Impl
	14. $(T \supset H) \cdot (H \supset T)$	6, 13, Conj
	15. $T \equiv H$	14, Equiv

Exercise 7.4
Part II

(2)	1. $(B \supset G) \cdot (F \supset N)$	
	2. $\sim(G \cdot N)$	/ $\sim(B \cdot F)$
	3. $\sim G \vee \sim N$	2, DM
	4. $(\sim G \supset \sim B) \cdot (\sim N \supset \sim F)$	1, Trans
	5. $\sim B \vee \sim F$	3, 4, CD
	6. $\sim(B \cdot F)$	5, DM

Exercise 7.4
Part II continued

(5)	1. $(O \supset C) \cdot (\sim S \supset \sim D)$	
	2. $(E \supset D) \cdot (\sim E \supset \sim C)$	/ $O \supset S$
	3. $O \supset C$	1, Simp
	4. $\sim S \supset \sim D$	1, Com, Simp
	5. $D \supset S$	4, Trans
	6. $E \supset D$	2, Simp
	7. $\sim E \supset \sim C$	2, Com, Simp
	8. $C \supset E$	7, Trans
	9. $O \supset E$	3, 8, HS
	10. $O \supset D$	6, 9, HS
	11. $O \supset S$	5, 10, HS

(8)	1. $S \vee \sim N$	
	2. $\sim S \vee Q$	/ $N \supset Q$
	3. $\sim N \vee S$	1, Com
	4. $N \supset S$	3, Impl
	5. $S \supset Q$	2, Impl
	6. $N \supset Q$	4, 5, HS

(11)	1. $\sim B \supset H$	
	2. $\sim D \supset H$	
	3. $\sim (B \cdot D)$	/ H
	4. $\sim B \vee \sim D$	3, DM
	5. $(\sim B \supset H) \cdot (\sim D \supset H)$	1, 2, Conj
	6. $H \vee H$	4, 5, CD
	7. H	6, Taut

(14)	1. $F \supset (A \cdot K)$	
	2. $G \supset (\sim A \cdot \sim K)$	
	3. $F \vee G$	/ $A \equiv K$
	4. $[F \supset (A \cdot K)] \cdot [G \supset (\sim A \cdot \sim K)]$	1, 2, Conj
	5. $(A \cdot K) \vee (\sim A \cdot \sim K)$	3, 4, CD
	6. $A \equiv K$	5, Equiv

(17)	1. $H \supset U$	/ $H \supset (U \vee T)$
	2. $\sim H \vee U$	1, Impl
	3. $(\sim H \vee U) \vee T$	2, Add
	4. $\sim H \vee (U \vee T)$	3, Assoc
	5. $H \supset (U \vee T)$	4, Impl

Exercise 7.4
Part II continued

(20)	1. $(G \supset J) \supset (H \supset Q)$	
	2. $J \cdot \sim Q$	/ $\sim H$
	3. J	2, Simp
	4. $J \vee \sim G$	3, Add
	5. $\sim G \vee J$	4, Com
	6. $G \supset J$	5, Impl
	7. $H \supset Q$	1, 6, MP
	8. $\sim Q$	2, Com, Simp
	9. $\sim H$	7, 8, MT

(23)	1. $(D \supset E) \supset (E \supset D)$	
	2. $(D \equiv E) \supset \sim(G \cdot \sim H)$	
	3. $E \cdot G$	/ $G \cdot H$
	4. E	3, Simp
	5. $E \vee \sim D$	4, Add
	6. $\sim D \vee E$	5, Com
	7. $D \supset E$	6, Impl
	8. $E \supset D$	1, 7, MP
	9. $(D \supset E) \cdot (E \supset D)$	7, 8, Conj
	10. $D \equiv E$	9, Equiv
	11. $\sim(G \cdot \sim H)$	2, 10, MP
	12. $\sim G \vee H$	11, DM, DN
	13. G	3, Com, Simp
	14. H	12, 13, DN, DS
	15. $G \cdot H$	13, 14, Conj

(26)	1. $A \equiv W$	
	2. $\sim A \vee \sim W$	
	3. $R \supset A$	/ $\sim(W \vee R)$
	4. $(A \cdot W) \vee (\sim A \cdot \sim W)$	1, Equiv
	5. $\sim(A \cdot W)$	2, DM
	6. $\sim A \cdot \sim W$	4, 5, DS
	7. $\sim A$	6, Simp
	8. $\sim R$	3, 7, MT
	9. $\sim W$	6, Com, Simp
	10. $\sim W \cdot \sim R$	8, 9, Conj
	11. $\sim(W \vee R)$	10, DM

Exercise 7.4
Part II continued

(29)	1. $O \supset (Q \cdot N)$	
	2. $(N \vee E) \supset S$	$/ O \supset S$
	3. $\sim O \vee (Q \cdot N)$	1, Impl
	4. $(\sim O \vee Q) \cdot (\sim O \vee N)$	3, Dist
	5. $\sim O \vee N$	4, Com, Simp
	6. $O \supset N$	5, Impl
	7. $\sim (N \vee E) \vee S$	2, Impl
	8. $(\sim N \cdot \sim E) \vee S$	7, DM
	9. $(\sim N \vee S) \cdot (\sim E \vee S)$	8, Com, Dist, Com
	10. $\sim N \vee S$	9, Simp
	11. $N \supset S$	10, Impl
	12. $O \supset S$	6, 11, HS

Exercise 7.4
Part III

(2)	1. $C \supset (D \cdot M)$	
	2. $\sim M$	$/ D \supset S$
	3. $\sim M \vee \sim D$	2, Add
	4. $\sim D \vee \sim M$	3, Com
	5. $\sim (D \cdot M)$	4, DM
	6. $\sim C$	1, 5, MP

(5)	1. $(E \vee P) \supset U$	$/ E \supset U$
	2. $\sim (E \vee P) \vee U$	1, Impl
	3. $(\sim E \cdot \sim P) \vee U$	2, DM
	4. $U \vee (\sim E \cdot \sim P)$	3, Com
	5. $(U \vee \sim E) \cdot (U \vee \sim P)$	4, Dist
	6. $U \vee \sim E$	5, Simp
	7. $\sim E \vee U$	6, Com
	8. $E \supset U$	7, Impl

Exercise 7.4
Part III, continued

(8)

	1. (S ⊃ (D · I)	
	2. S ∨ (U · D)	/ D
	3. ~S ∨ (D · I)	1, Impl
	4. (~S ∨ D) · (~S ∨ I)	3, Dist
	5. ~S ∨ D	4, Simp
	6. S ⊃ D	5, Impl
	7. (S ∨ U) · (S ∨ D)	2, Dist
	8. (S ∨ D) · (S ∨ U)	7, Com
	9. S ∨ D	8, Simp
	10. ~S ⊃ D	9, DN, Impl
	11. ~D ⊃ ~S	6, Trans
	12. ~D ⊃ D	10, 11, HS
	13. D ∨ D	12, Impl, DN
	14. D	13, Taut

Exercise 7.5
Part I

(2)

1. F ⊃ E		
2. (F · E) ⊃ R		/ F ⊃ R
	3. F	ACP
	4. E	1, 3, MP
	5. F · E	3, 4, Conj
	6. R	2, 5, MP
7. F ⊃ R		3-6, CP

(5)

1. A ⊃ ~(A ∨ E)		/ A ⊃ F
	2. A	ACP
	3. ~(A ∨ E)	1, 2, MP
	4. ~A · ~E	3, DM
	5. ~A	4, Simp
	6. A ∨ F	2, Add
	7. F	5, 6, DS
8. A ⊃ F		2-7, CP

Exercise 7.5
Part I, continued

(8)	1. $P \supset (Q \vee R)$	
	2. $(P \supset R) \supset (S \cdot T)$	
	3. $Q \supset R$	/ T
	4. P	ACP
	5. $Q \vee R$	1, 4, MP
	6. $R \vee Q$	5, Com
	7. $\sim R \supset Q$	6, DN, Impl
	8. $\sim R \supset R$	3, 7, HS
	9. $R \vee R$	8, Impl, DN
	10. R	9, Taut
	11. $P \supset R$	4-10, CP
	12. $S \cdot T$	2, 11, MP
	13. T	12, Com, Simp

(11)	1. $M \supset (K \supset L)$	
	2. $(L \vee N) \supset J$	/ $M \supset (K \supset J)$
	3. M	ACP
	4. K	ACP
	5. $K \supset L$	1, 3, MP
	6. L	4, 5, MP
	7. $L \vee N$	6, Add
	8. J	2, 7, MP
	9. $K \supset J$	4-8, CP
	10. $M \supset (K \supset J)$	3-9, CP

(14)	1. $(F \cdot G) \equiv H$	
	2. $F \supset G$	/ $F \equiv H$
	3. $[(F \cdot G) \supset H] \cdot [H \supset (F \cdot G)]$	1, Equiv
	4. F	ACP
	5. G	2, 4, MP
	6. $F \cdot G$	4, 5, Conj
	7. $(F \cdot G) \supset H$	3, Simp
	8. H	6, 7, MP
	9. $F \supset H$	4-8, CP
	10. H	ACP
	11. $H \supset (F \cdot G)$	3, Com, Simp
	12. $F \cdot G$	10, 11, MP
	13. F	12, Simp
	14. $H \supset F$	10-13, CP
	15. $(F \supset H) \cdot (H \supset F)$	9, 14, Conj
	16. $F \equiv H$	15, Equiv

Exercise 7.5
Part I, continued

(17)

	1. N ⊃ (O · P)	
	2. Q ⊃ (R · S)	/ (P ⊃ Q) ⊃ (N ⊃ S)
	3. P ⊃ Q	ACP
	4. N	ACP
	5. O · P	1, 4, MP
	6. P	5, Com, Simp
	7. Q	3, 6, MP
	8. R · S	2, 7, MP
	9. S	8, Com, Simp
	10. N ⊃ S	4-9, CP
	11. (P ⊃ Q) ⊃ (N ⊃ S)	3-10, CP

(20)

	1. A ⊃ [B ⊃ (C · ~D)]	
	2. (B ∨ E) ⊃ (D ∨ E)	/ (A · B) ⊃ (C · E)
	3. A · B	ACP
	4. A	3, Simp
	5. B ⊃ (C · D)	1, 4, MP
	6. B	3, Com, Simp
	7. C · ~D	5, 6, MP
	8. C	7, Simp
	9. ~D	7, Com, Simp
	10. B ∨ E	6, Add
	11. D ∨ E	2, 10, MP
	12. E	9, 11, DS
	13. C · E	8, 12, Conj
	14. (A · B) ⊃ (C · E)	3-13, CP

Exercise 7.5
Part II

(2) 1.

	1. P ⊃ (I ⊃ W)	
	2. I ⊃ (W ⊃ ~S)	/ P ⊃ (I ⊃ ~S)
	3. P	ACP
	4. I	ACP
	5. I ⊃ W	1, 3, MP
	6. W ⊃ ~S	2, 4, MP
	7. I ⊃ ~S	5, 6, HS
	8. ~S	4, 7, MP
	9. (H · U) ⊃ (S · D)	4-8, CP
	10. P ⊃ (I ⊃ ~S)	3-9, CP

Exercise 7.5
Part II, continued

(5)	1. $A \supset H$	
	2. $(F \vee W) \supset L$	/ $(H \supset F) \supset (A \supset L)$
	3. $H \supset F$	ACP
	4. A	ACP
	5. H	1, 4, MP
	6. F	3, 5, MP
	7. $F \vee W$	6, Add
	8. L	2, 7, MP
	9. $A \supset L$	4-8, CP
	10. $(H \supset F) \supset (A \supset L)$	3-9, CP

Exercise 7.6
Part I

(2)	1. $(K \supset K) \supset R$	
	2. $(R \vee M) \supset N$	/ N
	3. $\sim N$	AIP
	4. $\sim(R \vee M)$	2, 3, MT
	5. $\sim R \cdot \sim M$	4, DM
	6. $\sim R$	5, Simp
	7. $\sim(K \supset K)$	1, 6, MT
	8. $\sim(\sim K \vee K)$	7, Impl
	9. $K \cdot \sim K$	8, DM, DN
	10. N	3-9, IP, DN

(5)	1. $S \supset (T \vee \sim U)$	
	2. $U \supset (\sim T \vee R)$	
	3. $(S \cdot U) \supset \sim R$	/ $\sim S \vee \sim U$
	4. $\sim(\sim S \vee \sim U)$	AIP
	5. $S \cdot U$	4, DM, DN
	6. $\sim R$	3, 5, MP
	7. S	Simp
	8. U	6, Com, Simp
	9. $T \vee \sim U$	1, 7, MP
	10. $\sim T \vee R$	2, 8, MP
	11. $\sim T$	6, 10, Com, DS
	12. $\sim U$	9, 11, DS
	13. $U \cdot \sim U$	8, 12, Conj
	14. $\sim\sim(\sim S \vee \sim U)$	4-13, IP
	15. $\sim S \vee \sim U$	14, DN

(8)

1. ~M ⊃ (N · O)	
2. N ⊃ P	
3. O ⊃ ~P	/ M
4. ~M	AIP
5. N · O	1, 4, MP
6. N	5, Simp
7. P	2, 6, MP
8. ~O	3, 7, DN, MT
9. O	5, Com, Simp
10. O · ~O	8, 9, Conj
11. M	4-10, IP, DN

(11)

1. (A ∨ B) ⊃ C	
2. (~A ∨ D) ⊃ E	/ C ∨ E
3. ~C	ACP
4. ~(A ∨ B)	1, 3, MT
5. ~A · ~B	4, DM
6. ~A	5, Simp
7. ~A ∨ D	6, Add
8. E	2, 7, MP
9. ~C ⊃ E	3-8 CP
10. C ∨ E	9, Impl, DN

(14)

1. F	/(G ⊃ H) ∨ (~G ⊃ J)
2. G · ~H	ACP
3. G	2, Simp
4. G ∨ J	3, Add
5. ~G ⊃ J	4, DN, Impl
6. (G · ~H) ⊃ (~G ⊃ J)	2-5, CP
7. ~(G · ~H) ∨ (~G ⊃ J)	6, Impl
8. (~G ∨ H) ∨ (~G ⊃ J)	7, DM, DN
9. (G ⊃ H) ∨ (~G ⊃ J)	8, Impl

Exercise 7.6
Part I, continued

(17)

1.	R · S) ≡ (G · H)	
2.	R ⊃ S	
3.	H ⊃ G	/ R ≡ H
4.	[(R · S) ⊃ (G · H)] · [(G · H) ⊃ (R · S)]	1, Equiv
5.	R	ACP
6.	S	2, 5, MP
7.	R · S	5, 6, Conj
8.	(R · S) ⊃ (G · H)	4, Simp
9.	G · H	7, 8, MP
10.	H	9, Com, Simp
11.	R ⊃ H	5-10, CP
12.	H	ACP
13.	G	3, 12, MP
14.	G · H	12, 13, Conj
15.	(G · H) ⊃ (R · S)	4, Com, Simp
16.	R · S	14, 15, MP
17.	R	16, Simp
18.	H ⊃ R	12-17, CP
19.	(R ⊃ H) · (H ⊃ R)	11, 18, Conj
20.	R ≡ H	19, Equiv

(20)

1.	F ⊃ [(C ⊃ C) ⊃ G]	
2.	G ⊃ {[H ⊃ (E ⊃ H)] ⊃ (K · ~K)}	/ ~F
3.	F	AIP
4.	(C ⊃ C) ⊃ G	1, 3, MP
5.	C	ACP
6.	C ∨ C	5, Add
7.	C	6, Taut
8.	C ⊃ C	5-7, CP
9.	G	4, 8, MP
10.	[H ⊃ (E ⊃ H)] ⊃ (K · ~K)	2, 9, MP
11.	H	ACP
12.	H ∨ ~E	11, Add
13.	~E ∨ H	12, Com
14.	E ⊃ H	13, Impl
15.	H ⊃ (E ⊃ H)	11-14, CP
16.	K · ~K	10, 15, MP
17.	~F	3-16, IP

Exercise 7.6
Part II

(2)	1. $(C \vee R) \supset (N \cdot I)$	
	2. $(N \vee P) \supset (I \supset \sim C)$	/ $\sim C$
	3. C	AIP
	4. $C \vee R$	3, Add
	5. $N \cdot I$	1, 4, MP
	6. N	5, Simp
	7. $N \vee P$	6, Add
	8. $I \supset \sim C$	2, 7, MP
	9. I	5, Com, Simp
	10. $\sim C$	8, 9, MP
	11. $C \cdot \sim C$	3, 10, Conj
	12. $\sim C$	3-11, IP

(5)	1. $(B \cdot S) \vee (H \cdot C)$	
	2. $(P \vee H) \supset S$	
	3. $\sim S$	/ S
	4. $\sim(P \vee H)$	AIP
	5. $\sim P \cdot \sim H$	2, 3, MT
	6. $\sim H$	4, DM
	7. $\sim H \vee \sim C$	5, Com, Simp
	8. $\sim(H \cdot C)$	6, Add
	9. $(H \cdot C) \vee (B \cdot S)$	1, Com
	10. $B \cdot S$	8, 9, DS
	11. S	10, Com, Simp
	12. $S \cdot \sim S$	3, 11, Conj
	13. $\sim\sim S$	3-12 IP
	14. S	13, DN

Exercise 7.7

(2) / (~P ⊃ Q) ∨ (P ⊃ R)

1. ~[(~P ⊃ Q) ∨ (P ⊃ R)]	AIP
2. ~(~P ⊃ Q) · ~(P ⊃ R)	1, DM
3. ~(P ∨ Q) · ~(~P ∨ R)	2, Impl, DN
4. (~P · ~Q) · (P · ~R)	3, DM, DN
5. ~P · ~Q	4, Simp
6. P · ~R	4, Com, Simp
7. ~P	5, Simp
8. P	6, Simp
9. P · ~P	7, 8, Conj
10. (~P ⊃ Q) ∨ (P ⊃ R)	1-9, IP DN

(5) / (P ∨ ~Q) ⊃ [(~P ∨ R) ⊃ (Q ⊃ R)]

1. P ∨ ~Q	ACP
2. ~P ∨ R	ACP
3. ~Q ∨ P	1, Com
4. Q ⊃ P	3, Impl
5. P ⊃ R	2, Impl
6. Q ⊃ R	4, 5, HS
7. (~P ∨ R) ⊃ (Q ⊃ R)	2-6, CP
8. (P ∨ ~Q) ⊃ [(~P ∨ R) ⊃ (Q ⊃ R)]	1-7, CP

(8) / (P ⊃ Q) ≡ [P ⊃ (P · Q)]

1. P ⊃ Q	ACP
2. P	ACP
3. Q	1, 2, MP
4. P · Q	2, 3, Conj
5. P ⊃ (P · Q)	2-4, CP
6. (P ⊃ Q) ⊃ [P ⊃ (P · Q)]	1-5, CP
7. P ⊃ (P · Q)	ACP
8. P	ACP
9. P · Q	7, 8, MP
10. Q	9, Com, Simp
11. P ⊃ Q	8-10, CP
12. [P ⊃ (P · Q)] ⊃ (P ⊃ Q)	7-11, CP
13. {line 6]} · {line 12}	6, 12, Conj
14. (P ⊃ Q) ≡ [P ⊃ (P · Q)]	13, Equiv

Exercise 7.7, continued

(11) / [P ⊃ (Q ⊃ R)] ≡ [Q ⊃ (P ⊃ R)]

1. ~[(P ⊃ Q) ∨ (Q ⊃ P)]	AIP
2. ~(P ⊃ Q) · ~(Q ⊃ P)	1, DM
3. ~(~P ∨ Q) · ~(~Q ∨ P)	2, Impl
4. (P · ~Q) · (Q · ~P)	3, DM, DN
5. P · ~Q	4, Simp
6. Q · ~P	4, Com, Simp
7. P	5, Simp
8. ~P	6, Com, Simp
9. P · ~P	7, 8, Conj
10. (P ⊃ Q) ∨ (Q ⊃ P)	1-9, IP, DN

(14) / [(P ⊃ Q) ⊃ R] ⊃ [(R ⊃ ~R) ⊃ P]

1. (P ⊃ Q) ⊃ R	ACP
2. R ⊃ ~R	ACP
3. ~R ∨ ~R	2, Impl
4. ~R	3, Taut
5. ~(P ⊃ Q)	1, 4, MT
6. ~(~P ⊃ Q)	5, Impl
7. P · ~Q	6, DM, DN
8. P	7, Simp
9. (R ⊃ ~R) ⊃ P	2-8, CP
10. [(P ⊃ Q) ⊃ R] ⊃ [(R ⊃ ~R) ⊃ P]	1-9, CP

(17) / P ⊃ [(Q · ~Q) ⊃ R]

1. P	ACP
2. Q · ~Q	ACP
3. Q	2, Simp
4. Q ∨ R	3, Add
5. ~Q	2, Com, Simp
6. R	4, 5, DS
7. (Q · ~Q) ⊃ R	2-6, CP
8. P ⊃ [(Q · ~Q ⊃ R]	1-7, CP

Exercise 8.1

2. $(x)(Mx \supset Tx)$
5. $(\exists x)(Hx \cdot \sim Rx)$
8. $(\exists x)Tx$
11. $(\exists x)(Sx \cdot \sim Gx)$
14. $(x)(Sx \supset Vx)$
17. $(x)\sim Gx$
20. $(\exists x)(Mx \cdot \sim Ex)$
23. $(x)(Px \supset Gx)$
26. $(x)[(Wx \cdot Cx) \supset Rx]$
29. $(x)\ [(Vx \lor Cx) \supset (Sx \cdot Ix)]$
32. $(\exists x)[(Fx \cdot Rx) \cdot Ex]$
35. $(\exists x)(Wx \cdot Tx) \supset (Gp \lor Gh)$
38. $(x)[(Sx \lor Dx) \supset (Ix \cdot Ex)]$
41. $(x)[(Ex \cdot Mx) \supset Wx] \supset (x)[(Mx \cdot \sim Ex) \supset Lx]$
44. $(x)\{[(Px \lor Ax) \cdot Sx] \supset [(Cx \lor Rx) \supset Lx]\}$

Exercise 8.2
Part I

(2)	1. $(x)(Bx \supset Cx)$	
	2. $(\exists x)(Ax \cdot Bx)$	/ $(\exists x)(Ax \cdot Cx)$
	3. $Am \cdot Bm$	2, EI
	4. $Bm \supset Cm$	1, UI
	5. $Bm \cdot Am$	3, Com
	6. Bm	5, Simp
	7. Cm	4, 6, MP
	8. Am	3, Simp
	9. $Am \cdot Cm$	7, 8, Conj
	10. $(\exists x)(Ax \cdot Cx)$	8, EG

(5)	1. $(x)[(Ax \vee Bx) \supset Cx]$	
	2. $(\exists y)(Ay \cdot Dy)$	/ $(\exists y)Cy$
	3. $Am \cdot Dm$	2, EI
	4. Am	3, Simp
	5. $(Am \vee Bm) \supset Cm$	1, UI
	6. $Am \vee Bm$	4, Add
	7. Cm	5, 6, MP
	8. $(\exists y)Cy$	7, EG

(8)	1. $(x)(Ax \supset Bx)$	
	2. $Am \cdot An$	/ $Bm \cdot Bn$
	3. $Am \supset Bm$	1, UI
	4. Am	2, Simp
	5. Bm	3, 4, MP
	6. $An \supset Bn$	1, UI
	7. $An \cdot Am$	2, Com
	8. An	7, Simp
	9. Bn	6, 8, MP
	10. $Bm \cdot Bn$	5, 9, Conj

Exercise 8.2
Part I

(11)

	1. (x)[(Ax ∃ Bx) ⊃ Cx]	
	2. (∃x)(Bx · ~Cx)	/ (∃x)~Ax
	3. Bm · ~Cm	2, EI
	4. (Am · Bm) ⊃ Cm	1, UI
	5. ~Cm · Bm	3, Com
	6. ~Cm	5, Simp
	7. ~(Am · Bm)	4, 5, MT
	8. ~Am ∨ ~Bm	7, DM
	9. Bm	3, Simp
	10. ~Bm ∨ ~Am	8, Com
	11. ~Am	9, 10, DS
	12. (∃x)~Ax	11, EG

(14)

	1. (∃x)Ax ⊃ (x)(Cx ⊃ Bx)	
	2. (∃x)(Ax ∨ Bx)	
	3. (x)(Bx ⊃ Ax)	/ (x)(Cx ⊃ Ax)
	4. Am ∨ Bm	2, EI
	5. Bm ⊃ Am	3, UI
	6. ~Am ⊃ Bm	4, DN, Impl
	7. ~Am ⊃ Am	5, 6, HS
	8. Am ∨ Am	7, Impl, DN
	9. Am	8, Taut
	10. (∃x)Ax	9, EG
	11. (x)(Cx ⊃ Bx)	1, 10, MP
	12. Cx ⊃ Bx	11, UI
	13. Bx ⊃ Ax	3, UI
	14. Cx ⊃ Ax	12, 13, HS
	15. (x)(Cx ⊃ Ax)	14, UG

Exercise 8.2
Part II

(2)	1. (x)(Tx ⊃ Vx)	/ (x)[(Tx · Gx) ⊃ Vx]
	2. Tx ⊃ Vx	1, UI
	3. ~Tx v Vx	2, Impl
	4. Vx v ~Tx	3, Com
	5. (Vx v ~Tx) v ~Gx	4, Add
	6. Vx v (~Tx v ~Gx)	5, Assoc
	7. Vx v ~(Tx · Gx)	6, DM
	8. ~(Tx · Gx) v Vx	7, Com
	9. (Tx · Gx) ⊃ Vx	8, Impl
	10. (x)[(Tx · Gx) ⊃ Vx]	9, UG

(5)	1. (x)[(Bx v Px) ⊃ Lx]	
	2. (x)(Gx ⊃ ~Lx)	/ (x)(Gx ⊃ ~Bx)
	3. (Bx v Px) ⊃ Lx	1, UI
	4. Gx ⊃ ~Lx	2, UI
	5. ~Lx ⊃ ~(Bx v Px)	3, Trans
	6. Gx ⊃ ~(Bx v Px)	4, 5, HS
	7. Gx ⊃ (~Bx · ~Px)	6, DM
	8. ~Gx v (~Bx · ~Px)	7, Impl
	9. (~Gx v ~Bx) · (~Gx v ~Px)	8, Dist
	10. ~Gx v ~Bx	9, Simp
	11. Gx ⊃ ~Bx	10, Impl
	12. (x)(Gx ⊃ ~Bx)	11, UG

(8)	1. (∃x)(Hx · Rx)	
	2. (∃x)(Bx · Sx)	
	3. (∃x)Hx ⊃ (x)[Bx ⊃ (Sx ⊃ Ex)]	/ (∃x)(Bx · Ex)
	4. Hm · Rm	1, EI
	5. Bn · Sn	2, EI
	6. Hm	4, Simp
	7. (∃x)Hx	6, EG
	8. (x)[Bx ⊃ (Sx ⊃ Ex)]	3, 7, MP
	9. Bn ⊃ (Sn ⊃ En)	8, UI
	10. (Bn · Sn) ⊃ En	9, Exp
	11. En	5, 10, MP
	12. Bn	5, Simp
	13. Bn · En	11, 12, Conj
	14. (∃x)(Bx · Ex)	13, EG

Exercise 8.3
Part I

(2)

1.	$(\exists x) \sim Ax \vee (\exists x) \sim Bx$	
2.	$(x)Bx$	$/ \sim (x)Ax$
3.	$\sim (\exists x) \sim Bx$	2, CQ
4.	$(\exists x) \sim Ax$	1, 3, Com, DS
5.	$\sim (x)Ax$	4, CQ

(5)

1.	$(x)(Ax \cdot Bx) \vee (x)(Cx \cdot Dx)$	
2.	$\sim (x)Dx$	$/ (x)Bx$
3.	$(\exists x) \sim Dx$	2, CQ
4.	$\sim Dm$	3, EI
5.	$\sim Dm \vee \sim Cm$	4, Add
6.	$\sim Cm \vee \sim Dm$	5, Com
7.	$\sim (Cm \cdot Dm)$	6, DM
8.	$(\exists x) \sim (Cx \cdot Dx)$	7, EG
9.	$\sim (x)(Cx \cdot Dx)$	8, CQ
10.	$(x)(Ax \cdot Bx)$	1, 9, Com, DS
11.	$Ax \cdot Bx$	10, UI
12.	Bx	11, Com, Simp
13.	$(x)Bx$	12, UG

(8)

1.	$(x)Ax \supset (\exists x) \sim Bx$	
2.	$\sim (x)Bx \supset (\exists x) \sim Cx$	$/ (x)Cx \supset (\exists x) \sim Ax$
3.	$(x)Ax \supset \sim (x)Bx$	1, CQ
4.	$(x)Ax \supset (\exists x) \sim Cx$	2, 3, HS
5.	$\sim (\exists x) \sim Cx \supset \sim (x)Ax$	4, Trans
6.	$(x)Cx \supset (\exists x) \sim Ax$	5, CQ

(11)

1.	$\sim (\exists x)(Ax \cdot \sim Bx)$	
2.	$\sim (\exists x)(Ax \cdot \sim Cx)$	$/ (x)[Ax \supset (Bx \cdot Cx)]$
3.	$(x) \sim (Ax \cdot \sim Bx)$	1, CQ
4.	$(x) \sim (Ax \cdot \sim Cx)$	2, CQ
5.	$\sim (Ax \cdot \sim Bx)$	3, UI
6.	$\sim (Ax \cdot \sim Bx)$	4, UI
7.	$\sim Ax \vee Bx$	5, DM, DN
8.	$\sim Ax \vee Cx$	6, DM, DN
9.	$(\sim Ax \vee Bx) \cdot (\sim Ax \vee Cx)$	7, 8, Conj
10.	$\sim Ax \vee (Bx \cdot Cx)$	9, Dist
11.	$Ax \supset (Bx \cdot Cx)$	10, Impl
12.	$(x)[Ax \supset (Bx \cdot Cx)]$	11, UG

Exercise 8.3
Part I, continued

(14)

1.	$(\exists x) \sim Ax \supset (x) \sim Bx$	
2.	$(\exists x) \sim Ax \supset (\exists x)Bx$	
3.	$(x)(Ax \supset Cx)$	/ $(x)Cx$
4.	$\sim (x) \sim Bx \supset \sim (\exists x) \sim Ax$	1, Trans
5.	$(\exists x)Bx \supset \sim (\exists x) \sim Ax$	4, CQ
6.	$(\exists x) \sim Ax \supset \sim (\exists x) \sim Ax$	2, 5, HS
7.	$\sim (\exists x) \sim Ax \lor \sim (\exists x) \sim Ax$	6, Impl
8.	$\sim (\exists x) \sim Ax$	7, Taut
9.	$(x)Ax$	8, CQ
10.	Ax	9, UI
11.	$Ax \supset Cx$	3, UI
12.	Cx	10, 11, MP
13.	$(x)Cx$	12, UG

Exercise 8.3
Part II

(2)

1.	$Ia \lor (x)(Px \supset Ix)$	
2.	$\sim (\exists x)Ix$	/ $\sim Pa$
3.	$(x) \sim Ix$	2, CQ
4.	$\sim Ia$	3, UI
5.	$(x)(Px \supset Ix)$	1, 4, DS
6.	$Pa \supset Ia$	5, UI
7.	$\sim Pa$	4, 6, MT

(5)

1.	$(x)[(Px \cdot \sim Ax) \supset Ix]$	
2.	$\sim (\exists x)(Px \cdot Ix)$	/ $(x)(Px \supset Ax)$
3.	$(x) \sim (Px \cdot Ix)$	2, CQ
4.	$\sim (Px \cdot Ix)$	3, UI
5.	$\sim Px \lor \sim Ix$	4, DM
6.	$\sim Ix \lor \sim Px$	5, Com
7.	$Ix \lor \sim Px$	6, Impl
8.	$(Px \cdot \sim Ax) \supset Ix$	1, UI
9.	$(Px \cdot \sim Ax) \supset \sim Px$	7, 8, HS
10.	$(\sim Ax \cdot Px) \supset \sim Px$	9, Com
11.	$\sim Ax \supset (Px \supset \sim Px)$	10, Exp
12.	$\sim Ax \supset (\sim Px \lor \sim Px)$	11, Impl
13.	$\sim Ax \supset \sim Px$	12, Taut
14.	$Px \supset Ax$	13, Trans
15.	$(x)(Px \supset Ax)$	14, UG

Exercise 8.3
Part II, continued

(8)

1.	(∃x)(Ox · ~Gx) ⊃ (∃x)(Hx · Rx)	
2.	~(∃x)(Hx ∨ Gx)	/ ~(∃x)Ox
3.	(x)~(Hx ∨ Gx)	2, CQ
4.	~(Hx ∨ Gx)	3, UI
5.	~Hx · ~Gx	4, DM
6.	~Hx	5, Simp
7.	~Hx ∨ ~Rx	6, Add
8.	~(Hx · Rx)	7, DM
9.	(x)~(Hx · Rx)	8, UG
10.	~(∃x)(Hx · Rx)	9, CQ
11.	~(∃x)(Ox · ~Gx)	1, 10, MT
12.	(x)~(Ox · ~Gx)	11, CQ
13.	~(Ox · ~Gx)	12, UI
14.	~Ox ∨ Gx	13, DM, DN
15.	~Gx	5, Com, Simp
16.	~Ox	14, 15, Com, DS
17.	(x)~Ox	16, UI
18.	~(∃x)Ox	17, CQ

Exercise 8.4
Part I

(2)

1.	(∃x)(Ax ⊃ (∃x)(Bx · Cx)	
2.	(∃x)(Cx ∨ Dx) ⊃ (x)Ex	/ (x)(Ax ⊃ Ex)
3.	Ax	ACP
4.	(∃x)Ax	3, EG
5.	(∃x)(Bx · Cx)	1, 4, MP
6.	Bm · Cm	5, EI
7.	Cm	6, Com, Simp
8.	Cm ∨ Dm	7, Add
9.	(∃x)(Cx ∨ Dx)	8, EG
10.	(x)Ex	2, 9, MP
11.	Ex	10, UI
12.	Ax ⊃ Ex	3-11, CP
13.	(x)(Ax ⊃ Ex)	12, UG

Exercise 8.4
Part I, continued

(5)	1. (x)(Ax ⊃ Bx)	
	2. (x)[(Ax · Bx) ⊃ Cx]	/ (x)(Ax ⊃ Cx)
	3. Ax	ACP
	4. Ax ⊃ Bx	1, UI
	5. (Ax · Bx) ⊃ Cx	2, UI
	6. Bx	3, 4, MP
	7. Ax · Bx	3, 6, Conj
	8. Cx	5, 7, MP
	9. Ax ⊃ Cx	3-8, CP
	10. (x)(Ax ⊃ Cx)	9, UG

(8)	1. (∃x)(Ax ∨ Bx) ⊃ ~(∃x)Ax	/ (x)~Ax
	2. ~(x)~Ax	AIP
	3. (∃x)Ax	2, CQ
	4. Am	3, EI
	5. Am ∨ Bm	4, Add
	6. (∃x)(Ax ∨ Bx)	5, EG
	7. ~(∃x)Ax	1, 6, MP
	8. (x)~Ax	7, CQ
	9. ~Am	8, UI
	10. Am · ~Am	4, 9, Conj
	11. (x)~Ax	2-10, IP, DN

(11)	1. (x)[(Ax ∨ Bx) ⊃ Cx]	
	2. (x)[(Cx ∨ Dx) ⊃ ~Ax] / (x)~Ax	
	3. ~(x)~Ax	AIP
	4. (∃x)Ax	3, CQ
	5. Am	4, EI
	6. (Am ∨ Bm) ⊃ Cm	1, UI
	7. Am ∨ Bm	5, Add
	8. Cm	6, 7, MP
	9. (Cm ∨ Dm) ⊃ ~Am	2, UI
	10. Cm ∨ Dm	8, Add
	11. ~Am	9, 10, MP
	12.Am · ~Am	5, 11, Conj
	13. (x)~Ax	3-12, IP, DN

Exercise 8.4
Part I, continued

(14)

1. (∃x)Ax ∨ (∃x)(Bx · Cx)	
2. (x)(Ax ⊃ Cx)	/ (∃x)Cx
3. ~(∃x)Cx	AIP
4. (x)~Cx	3, CQ
5. ~Cx	4, UI
6.Ax ⊃ Cx	2, UI
7. ~Ax	5,6, MT
8. (x)~Ax	7, UG
9. ~(∃x)Ax	8, CQ
10. (∃x)(Bx · Cx)	1,9, DS
11. Bm · Cm	10, EI
12. Cm	11, Com, Simp
13. ~Cm	4, UI
14. Cm · ~Cm	12,13, Conj
15. (∃x)Cx	3-14, IP, DN

(17)

1. (x)Ax ≡ (∃x)(Bx · Cx)	
2. (x)(Cx ⊃ Bx)	. / (x)Ax ≡ (∃x)Cx
3. [(x)Ax ⊃ (∃x)(Bx · Cx)] · [(∃x)(Bx · Cx) ⊃ (x)Ax]	1, Equiv
4. (x)Ax	ACP
5. (x)Ax ⊃ (∃x)(Bx · Cx)	3, Simp
6. (∃x)(Bx · Cx)	4, 5, MP
7. Bm ·Cm	6, EI
8. Cm	7, Com, Simp
9. (∃x)Cx	8, EG
10. (x)Ax ⊃ (∃x)Cx	4-9, CP
11. (∃x)Cx	ACP
12. Cn	11, EI
13. Cn ⊃ Bn	2, UI
14. Bn12,	13, MP
15. Bn · Cn	12,14, Conj
16. (∃x)(Bx ·Cx) ⊃ (x)Ax	15, EG
17. (∃x)(Bx ·Cx) ⊃ (x)Ax]	3, Com, Simp
18. (x)Ax	16, 17, MP
19. (∃x)Cx ⊃ (x)Ax	11-18, CP
20. [(x)Ax ⊃ (∃x)Cx] · [(∃x)x ⊃ (x)Ax]	10, 19, Conj
21. (x)Ax ≡ (∃x)Cx	20, Equiv

Exercise 8.4
Part I, continued

(20)

1.	(x)[Ax ⊃ (Bx · Cx)]	
2.	(x)[Dx ⊃ (Ex · Fx)]	/ (x)(Cx ⊃ Dx) ⊃ (x)(Ax ⊃ Fx)
3.	(x)(Cx ⊃ Dx)	ACP
4.	Ax	ACP
5.	Ax ⊃ (Bx · Cx)	1, UI
6.	Bx · Cx	4, 5, MP
7.	Cx	6, Com, Simp
8.	Cx ⊃ Dx	3, UI
9.	Dx	7, 8, MP
10.	Dx ⊃ (Ex · Fx)	2, UI
11.	Ex · Fx	9, 10, MP
12.	Fx	11, Com, Simp
13.	Ax ⊃ Fx	4-12, CP
14.	(x)(Ax ⊃ Fx)	13, UG
15.	(x)(Cx ⊃ Dx) ⊃ (X)(Ax ⊃ Fx)	3-14, CP

Exercise 8.4
Part II

(2)

1.	(x)(Sx ⊃ Wx)	
2.	(∃x)(Wx · Sx) ⊃ Vo	/ (∃x)Sx ⊃ Vo
3.	(∃x)Sx	ACP
4.	Sm	3, EI
5.	Sm ⊃ Wm	1, UI
6.	Wm	4, 5, MP
7.	Wm · Sm	4, 6, Conj
8.	(∃x)(Wx · Sx)	7, EG
9.	Vo	2, 8, MP
10.	(∃x)Sx ⊃ Vo	3-9, CP

Exercise 8.4
Part II, continued

(5)

1. (x)(Ax ⊃ Dx)	
2. (x)[(Ex · Ax) ⊃ Cx] · (x)[(Cx · Dx) ⊃ Fx]	/ (x)[(Ex · Ax) ⊃ Fx]
3. Ex · Ax	ACP
4. (x)[(Ex · Ax) ⊃ Cx]	2, Simp
5. (x)[(Cx · Dx) ⊃ Fx]	2, Com, Simp
6. (Ex · Ax) ⊃ Cx	4, UI
7. (Cx · Dx) ⊃ Fx	5, UI
8. Cx	3, 6, MP
9. Ax	3, Com, Simp
10. Ax ⊃ Dx	1, UI
11. Dx	9, 10, MP
12. Cx · Dx	8, 11, Conj
13. Fx	7, 12, MP
14. (Ex · Ax) ⊃ Fx	3-13, CP
15. (x)[(Ex · Ax) ⊃ Fx]	14, UG

(8)

1. (∃x)Vx ⊃ (x)(Px ⊃ Ax)	
2. (∃x)Px ⊃ (x)(Ax ⊃ Cx)	/(∃x)Vx ⊃ (x)(Px ⊃ Cx)
3. (∃x)Vx	ACP
4. Px	ACP
5. (x)(Px ⊃ Ax)	1, 3, MP
6. (∃x)Px	4, EG
7. (x)(Ax ⊃ Cx)	2, 6, MP
8. Px ⊃ Ax	5, UI
9. Ax	4, 8, MP
10. Ax ⊃ Cx	7, UI
11. Cx	9, 10, MP
12. Px ⊃ Cx	4-11, CP
13. (x)(Px ⊃ Cx)	12, UG
14. (∃x)Vx ⊃ (x)(Px ⊃ Cx)	3-13, CP

Exercise 8.5
Part I

2. Some animals are fish.
All cats are animals.
Therefore, some cats are fish.

Exercise 8.5
Part I, continued

5. Everything is either animal, vegtable or mineral.
Therefore, either everything is an animal, or everything is a vegetable or everything is a mineral.

8. Anything tha is either a dog or a cat is an animal.
Any animal that has a trunk is an elephant.
Therefore, all dogs are elephants.

Exercise 8.5
Part II

(2) 1. (x)(Ax ∨ Bx)
2. ~An / (x)Bx

For a universe consisting of two members, we have,

(An ∨ Bn) · (Aa ∨ Ba) / ~ An // Bn · Ba
F T TT T T F T F T F F

(5) 1. (x)[Ax ⊃ (Bx ∨ Cx)]
2. (∃x)Ax / (∃x)Bx

For a universe consisting of one member, we have,

Aa ⊃ (Ba ∨ Ca) / Aa // Ba
T T F T T T F

(8) 1. (∃x)(Ax · Bx) ≡ (∃x)Cx
2. (x)(Ax ⊃ Bx) / (x)Ax ≡ (∃x)Cx

For a universe consisting of two members, we have,

[(Aa · Ba) ∨ (Ab · Bb)] ≡ (Ca ∨ Cb) / (Aa ⊃ Ba) · (Ab ⊃ Bb)
T T T T F F F T T T T T T F T F

// (Aa · Ab) ≡ (Ca ∨ Cb)
T F F F T T

Exercise 8.5
Part III

(2) 1. (x)[(Px ∨ Hx) ⊃ Mx]
2. Pa / (x)Mx

For a universe consisting of two members, we have,

```
[(Pa ∨ Ha) ⊃ Ma] · [(Pc ∨ Hc) ⊃ Mc] / Pa // Ma · Mc
  T T      T T   T  F FF   T    F  T    T  F   F
```

(5) 1. (x)[(Cx ∨ Vx) ⊃ Mx]
2. (∃x)(Vx · ~Cx)
3. (∃x)(Vx · ~Vx) / (x)Mx

For a universe consisting of three members, we have,

```
{[(Ca ∨ Va) ⊃ Ma] · [(Cb ∨ Vb) ⊃ Mb]} · [(Cc ∨ Vc) ⊃ Mc]
   T  T   F  T  T T  F  T   TT    T  T  F  F   F T  F

/[Va · ~ Ca) ∨ (Vb · ~ Cb)] ∨ (Vc · ~ Cc)
  F  FF  TT   T  TT   F   T  F  FT   F

/ [(Ca · ~ Va) ∨ (Cb · ~ Vb)] ∨ (Cc · ~ Vc)
    T  T TF     T  F  FF   T   T  F  FT   F

// (Ma · Mb) · Mc
    T   T   TF  F
```

Exercise 8.6
Part I

2. (x)(Rxp ⊃ Ex)

5. (x)(Tjx ⊃ Gx)

8. (∃x)[Px · (y)~Sxy]

11. (x)[(Dx · Srx) ⊃ Gx] (assuming the hotel also serves food)
(x)[Srx ⊃ (Gx · Dx)] (assuming the hotel serves no food)

14. (x)[(Cx · Lx) · Dpx]

Exercise 8.6
Part I, continued

17. (∃x)[Px · (y)(Ixy ⊃ Bxy)]

20. (∃x){Px · (y)[(Py · Mxy) ⊃ Axy]}

23. (∃x)Cx ⊃ (∃x)(Cx · Px)

26. (∃x){Lx · (y)[(Py · ~Ryy) ⊃ Rxy]}

29. (x){(Sx · Dx) ⊃ [(y)(Ty ⊃ ~By) ⊃ Hx]}

Exercise 8.6
Part II

(2)

1. (x)[Ax ⊃ (y)(By ⊃ Cxy)]	
2. Am · Bn	/ Cmn
3. Am ⊃ (y)(By ⊃ Cmy)	1, UI
4. Am	2, Simp
5.(y)(By ⊃ Cmy)	3, 4, MP
6. Bn ⊃ Cmn	5, UI
7. Bn	2, Com, Simp
8. Cmn	6, 7, MP

(5)

1. (∃x)Ax ⊃ (∃y)By	/ (∃y)(x)(Ax ⊃ By)
2. Ax	ACP
3. (∃x)Ax	2, EG
4. (∃y)By	1, 3, MP
5. Bm	4, EI
6. Ax ⊃ Bm	2-5, CP
7. (x)(Ax ⊃ Bm)	6, UG
8. (∃y)(x)(Ax ⊃ By)	7, EG

Exercise 8.6
Part II, continued

(8)

1.	(∃x)[Ax · (y)(By ⊃ Cxy)]	
2.	(x)(∃y)(Ax ⊃ By)	/ (∃x)(∃y)Cxy
3.	Am · (Y)(By ⊃ Cmy)	1, EI
4.	Am	3, Simp
5.	(y)(By ⊃ Cmy)	3, Com, Simp
6.	(∃y)(Am ⊃ By)	2, UI
7.	Am ⊃ Bn	6, EI
8.	Bn	4, 7, MP
9.	Bn ⊃ Cmn	5, UI
10.	Cmn	8, 9, MP
11.	(∃y)Cmy	10, EG
12.	(∃x)(∃y)Cxy	11, EG

(11)

1.	(∃x){Ax · [(∃y)By ⊃ Cx]}	
2.	(x)(Ax ⊃ Bx)	/ (∃x)Cx
3.	Am · [(∃y)By ⊃ Cm]	1, EI
4.	Am	3, Simp
5.	Am ⊃ Bm	2, UI
6.	Bm	4, 5, MP
7.	(∃y)By	6, EG
8.	(∃y)By ⊃ Cm	3, Com, Simp
9.	Cm	7, 8, MP
10.	(∃x)Cx	9, EG

(14)

1.	(x){Ax ⊃ [(∃y)(By · Cy) ⊃ Dx]}	
2.	(x)(Bx ⊃ Cx)	/ (x)[Ax ⊃ (Bx ⊃ Dx)]
3.	Ax	ACP
4.	Bx	ACP
5.	Ax ⊃ [(∃y)(By · Cy) ⊃ Dx]	1, UI
6.	(∃y)(By · Cy) ⊃ Dx	3, 5, MP
7.	Bx ⊃ Cx	2, UI
8.	Cx	4, 7, MP
9.	Bx · Cx	4, 8, Conj
10.	(∃y)(By · Cy)	9, EG
11.	Dx	6, 10, MP
12.	Bx ⊃ Dx	4-11, CP
13.	Ax ⊃ (Bx ⊃ Dx)	3-12, CP
14.	(x)[Ax ⊃ (Bx ⊃ Dx)]	13, UG

Exercise 8.6
Part II, continued

(17)

1.	(x)(∃y)(Ax ∨ By)	/ (∃y)(x)(Ax ∨ By)
2.	~(∃y)(x)(Ax ∨ By)	AIP
3.	(y)~(x)(Ax ∨ By)	2, CQ
4.	(y)(∃x)~(Ax ∨ By)	3, CQ
5.	(∃x)~(Ax ∨ By)	4, UI
6.	~(Am · By)	5, EI
7.	~Am · ~By	6, DM
8.	(∃y)(Am ∨ By)	1, UI
9.	Am ∨ Bn	8, EI
10.	~Am	7, Simp
11.	Bn	9, 10, DS
12.	~By	7, Com, Simp
13.	(y)~By	12, UG
14.	~Bn	13, UI
15.	Bn · ~Bn	11, 14, Conj
16.	(∃y)(x)(Ax ∨ By)	2-15, IP, DN

(Note: Attempts to use direct proof on this argument violate the second restruction on UG.)

(20)

1.	(x)(y)[Axy ⊃ (Bx · Cy)]	
2.	(x)(y)[(Bx ∨ Dy) ⊃ ~Axy]	/ ~(∃x)(∃y)Axy
3.	(∃x)(∃y)Axy	AIP
4.	(∃y)Amy	3, EI
5.	Amn	4, EI
6.	(y)[Amy ⊃ (Bm · Cy)]	1, UI
7.	Amn ⊃ (Bm · Cn)	6, UI
8.	Bm · Cn	5, 7, MP
9.	Bm	8, Simp
10.	(y)[Bm ∨ Dy) ⊃ ~Amy]	2, UI
11.	(Bm ∨ Dn) ⊃ ~Amn	10, UI
12.	Bm ∨ Dn	9, Add
13.	~Amn	11, 12, MP
14.	Amn · ~Amn	5, 13, Conj
15.	~(∃x)(∃y)Axy	3-14, IP

Exercise 8.6
Part III

(2)

1. $(x)[(Fxm \vee Fxp) \supset Rx]$	
2. $(\exists x)Fxm \supset Fem$	/ $Fam \supset Re$
3. Fam	ACP
4. $(\exists x)Fxm$	3, EG
5. Fem	2, 4, MP
6. $(Fem \vee Fep) \supset Re$	1, UI
7. $Fem \vee Fep$	5, Add
8. Re	6, 7, MP
9. $Fam \supset Re$	3-8, CP

(5)

1. $(x)\{(Hx \cdot Px) \supset [(y)(By \supset Cy) \supset Rx]\}$	
2. $(\exists x)[(Hx \cdot Px) \cdot \sim Rx]$	/ $(\exists x)(Bx \cdot \sim Cx)$
3. $(Hm \cdot Pm) \cdot \sim Rm$	2, EI
4. $Hm \cdot Pm$	3, Simp
5. $(Hm \cdot Pm) \supset [(y)(By \supset Cy) \supset Rm\}$	1, UI
6. $(y)(By \supset Cy) \supset Rm$	4, 5, MP
7. $\sim Rm$	3, Com, Simp
8. $\sim (y)(By \supset Cy)$	6, 7, MT
9. $(\exists y) \sim (By \supset Cy)$	8, CQ
10. $\sim (Bn \supset Cn)$	9, EI
11. $\sim (\sim Bn \vee Cn)$	10, Impl
12. $Bn \cdot \sim Cn$	11, Dm, DN
13. $(\exists x)(Bx \cdot \sim Cx)$	12, EG

(8)

1. $(x)[Px \supset (y)(Ry \supset Axy)]$	
2. $(x)\{Rx \cdot (\exists y)(Py \cdot Ayx)] \supset Jx\}$	
3. $(\exists x)Px \cdot Rm$	/ Jm
4. $(\exists x)Px$	3, Simp
5. Pc	4, EI
6. $Pc \supset (y)(Ry \supset Acy)$	1, UI
7. $(y)(Ry \supset Acy)$	5, 6, MP
8. $Rm \supset Acm$	7, UI
9. Rm	3, Com, Simp
10. Acm	8, 9, MP
11. $[Rm \cdot (\exists y)(Py \cdot Aym)] \supset Jm$	2, UI
12. $Pc \cdot Acm$	5, 10, Conj
13. $(\exists y)(Py \cdot Aym)$	12, EG
14. $Rm \cdot (\exists y)(Py \cdot Aym)$	9, 13, Conj
15. Jm	11, 14, MP

Exercise 8.7
Part I

Simple identity statements:

2. $r \neq m$

Statements involving "only," "the only," and "no except":

2. $P1 \cdot (x)(Px \supset x = 1)$
5. $Uw \cdot Fw \cdot Ua \cdot Fa \cdot (x)[(Ux \cdot Fx) \supset (x = w \vee x = a)]$

Superlative statements:

2. $Pp \cdot (x)[(Px \cdot x \neq p) \supset Spx]$

Statements involving "all except":

2. $Uf \cdot \sim Wf \cdot (x)[(Ux \cdot x \neq f) \supset Wx]$

Numerical statements:

2. $(x)(y)(z)(Nx \cdot Sx \cdot Ny \cdot Sy \cdot Nz \cdot Sz) \supset (x = y \vee x = z \vee y = z)]$
5. $(\exists x)(Qx \cdot Fx)$
8. $(\exists x)[Ux \cdot (y)(Uy \supset y = x)]$

Statements containing definite descriptions:

2. $(\exists x)[Wxo \cdot (y)(Wyo \supset y = x) \cdot x = d]$

Assorted statements:

2. $(\exists x)(Nx \cdot Sx)$
5. $(\exists x)(\exists y)(Cx \cdot Qx \cdot Cy \cdot Qy \cdot x \neq y)$
8. $Bd \cdot Md \cdot \sim Rd \cdot (x)[(Bx \cdot Mx \cdot x \neq d) \supset Rx]$
11. $(\exists x)\{Ex \cdot Dxn \cdot (y)[(Ey \cdot Dyn) \supset y = x] \cdot x = a\}$
14. $Pj \cdot Rj \cdot \sim Ij \cdot (x)[(Px \cdot Rx \cdot x \neq j) \supset Ix]$

Exercise 8.7
Part II

(2)

1. $Ur \cdot (x)[(Ux \cdot x \neq r) \supset Orx]$	
2. Uw	
3. $w \neq r$	/ Orw
4. $(x)[(Ux \cdot x \neq r) \supset Orx$	1, Com, Simp
5. $(Uw \cdot w \neq r) \supset Orw$	4, UI
6. $Uw \cdot w \neq r$	2, 3, Conj
7. Orw	5, 6, MP

(5)

1. $(\exists x)[Wxk \cdot (y)(Wyk \supset y = x) \cdot Ex \cdot Ax]$	
2. $Em \cdot \sim Am$	/ ~ Wmk
3. $Wak \cdot (y)(Wyk \supset y = a) \cdot Ea \cdot Aa$	1, EI
4. $(y)(Wyk \supset y = a)$	3, Com, Simp
5. $Wmk \supset m = a$	4, UI
6. Wmk	5, AIP
7. $m = a$	5, 6, MP
8. Aa	3, Com, Simp
9. $A = m$	7, Id
10. Am	8, 9, Id
11. $\sim Am$	2, Com, Simp
12. $Am \cdot \sim Am$	10, 11, Conj
13. $\sim Wmk$	6-12, IP

(8)

1. $Pa \cdot Oa \cdot (y)[(Py \cdot Oy) \supset y = a]$	
2. $Pw \cdot Sw \cdot (y)[(Py \cdot Sy) \supset y = w]$	
3. $(\exists x)(Px \cdot Ox \cdot Sx)$	/ a = w
4. $Pc \cdot Oc \cdot Sc$	3, EI
5. $(y)(Py \cdot Oy) \supset y = a$	1, Com, Simp
6. $(Pc \cdot Oc) \supset c = a$	5, UI
7. $Pc \cdot Oc$	4, Simp
8. $c = a$	6, 7, MP
9. $(y)[(Py \cdot Sy) \supset y = w]$	2, Com, Simp
10. $(Pc \cdot Sc) \supset c = w$	9, UI
11. $Pc \cdot Sc$	4, Com, Simp
12. $c = w$	10, 11, MP
13. $a = c$	8, Id
14. $a = w$	12, 13, Id

Exercise 8.7
Part II, continued

(11)

1. $(\exists x)(\exists y)(Px \cdot Lx \cdot Py \cdot Ly \cdot x \neq y)$	
2. $Pr \cdot Fr \cdot Lr \cdot (y)[(Py \cdot Fy \cdot Ly) \supset y = r]$	/ $(\exists x)(Px \cdot Lx \cdot \sim Fx)$
3. $\sim(\exists x)(Px \cdot Lx \cdot \sim Fx)$	AIP
4. $(\exists x)(Px \cdot Lx \cdot \sim Fx)$	1, EI
5. $Pa \cdot La \cdot Pc \cdot Lc \cdot a \neq c$	4, EI
6. $(y)[(Py \cdot Fy \cdot Ly) \supset y = r]$	2, Com, Simp
7. $(Pa \cdot Fa \cdot La) \supset a = r$	6, UI
8. $(Pc \cdot Fc \cdot Lc) \supset c = r$	6, UI
9. $(x)\sim(Px \cdot Lx \cdot \sim Fx)$	3, CQ
10. $\sim(Pa \cdot La \cdot \sim Fa)$	9, UI
11. $\sim(Pa \cdot La) \vee Fa$	10, DM, DN
12. $Pa \cdot La$	5, Com
13. Fa	11, 12, DN, DS
14. $Pa \cdot Fa \cdot La$	12, 13, Conj, Com
15. $a = r$	7, 14, MP
16. $\sim(Pc \cdot Lc \cdot \sim Fc)$	9, UI
17. $\sim(Pc \cdot Lc) \vee Fc$	16, DM, DN
18. $Pc \cdot Lc$	5, Com, Simp
19. Fc	17, 18, DN, DS
20. $Pc \cdot Fc \cdot Lc$	18, 19, Conj, Com
21. $c = r$	8, 20, MP
22. $r = c$	21, Id
23. $a = c$	15, 22, Id
24. $a \neq c$	5, Com, Simp
25. $a = c \cdot a \neq c$	23, 24, Conj
26. $(\exists x)(Px \cdot Lx \sim Fx)$	3-25, IP

Exercise 8.7
Part II, continued

(14)

1.	$(x)(y)(z)[(Sx \cdot Lx \cdot Ly \cdot Sz \cdot Lz) \supset (x = y \lor x = z \lor y = z)]$	
2.	$(\exists x)(\exists y)(Sx \cdot Lx \cdot Rx \cdot Sy \cdot Ly \cdot Ry \cdot x \neq y)$	
3.	$(x)(Rx \supset \sim Cx)$	/ $(Sn \cdot Cn) \supset \sim Ln$
4.	$(\exists y)(Sa \cdot La \cdot Ra \cdot Sy \cdot Ly \cdot Ry \cdot a \neq y)$	2, EI
5.	$Sa \cdot La \cdot Ra \cdot Sc \cdot Lc \cdot Rc \cdot a \neq c$	4, EI
6.	$(y)(z)[(Sa \cdot La \cdot Sy \cdot Ly \cdot Sz \cdot Lz) \supset (a = y \lor a = z \lor y = z)]$	1, UI
7.	$(z)[(Sa \cdot La \cdot Sc \cdot Lc \cdot Sz \cdot Lz) \supset (a = c \lor a = z \lor c = z)]$	6, UI
8.	$(Sa \cdot La \cdot Sc \cdot Lc \cdot Sn \cdot Ln) \supset (a = c \lor a = n \lor c = n)$	7, UI
9.	$Sn \cdot Cn \cdot Ln$	AIP
10.	$Sn \cdot Ln$	9, Com, Simp
11.	$Sa \cdot La$	5, Simp
12.	$Sc \cdot Lc$	5, Com, Simp
13.	$Sa \cdot La \cdot Sc \cdot Lc \cdot Sn \cdot Ln$	10-12, Conj
14.	$a = c \lor a = n \lor c = n$	8, 13, MP
15.	$a \neq c$	5, Com, Simp
16.	$a = n \lor c = n$	14, 15, DS
17.	$Ra \supset \sim Ca$	3, UI
18.	Ra	5, Com, Simp
19.	$\sim Ca$	17, 18, MP
20.	$a = n$	AIP
21.	$\sim Cn$	19, 20, Id
22.	Cn	9, Com, Simp
23.	$Cn \cdot \sim Cn$	21, 22, Conj
24.	$a \neq n$	20-23, IP
25.	$c = n$	16, 24, DS
26.	$Rc \supset \sim Cc$	3, UI
27.	Rc	5, Com, Simp
28.	$\sim Cc$	26, 27, MP
29.	$\sim Cn$	25, 28, Id
30.	Cn	9, Com, Simp
31.	$Cn \cdot \sim Cn$	29, 30, Conj
32.	$\sim(Sn \cdot Cn \cdot Ln)$	9-31, IP
33.	$\sim(Sn \cdot Cn) \lor \sim Ln$	32, DM
34.	$(Sn \cdot Cn) \supset \sim Ln$	33, Impl

Exercise 9.3, I.

2. Prob(A) = 273/9750
5. Prob(A) = 2/52

Exercise 9.3, II.

2. Use restricted conjunction rule.
P(H1 and H2 and H3) = P(H1) x P(H2) x P(H3) =
1/2 x 1/2 x 1/2 = 1/8
3. Use restricted disjunction rule.
P(K or Q) = P(K) + P(Q) = 4/52 + 4/52 = 8/52
4a. Use restricted conjunction rule.
P(A1 and A2) = P(A1) x P(A2) = 4/52 x 4/52 = 16/2704
4b. Use general conjunction rule.
P(A1 and A2) = P(A1) x P(A2 given A1) =
4/52 x 3/51 = 12/2652
5. P(A1 or A2) = P(A1) + P(A2) - P(A1 and A2) =
4/52 + 4/52 - (4/52 x 4/52) = 8/52 - 16/2704 = 400/2704
8.a. P(5) = P(1 and 4) + P(2 and 3) + P(3 and 2) + P(4 and 1) = (1/6 x 1/6) + (1/6 x 1/6) + (1/6 x 1/6) + (1/6 x 1/6) = 4/36
b. P(6) = P(1 and 5) + P(2 and 4) + P(3 and 3) + P(4 and 2) + P(5 and 1) = (1/6 x 1/6) + (1/6 x 1/6) + (1/6 x 1/6) + (1/6 x 1/6) + (1/6 x 1/6) = 5/36
c. P(7) = P(1 and 6) + P(2 and 5) + P(3 and 4) +P(4 and 3) + P(5 and 2) + P(6 and 1) = (1/6 x 1/6) + (1/6 x 1/6) + (1/6 x 1/6) + (1/6 x 1/6) + (1/6 x 1/6) + (1/6 x 1/6) = 6/36
9a. P(R1 and R2) = P(R1) x P(R2) = 2/9 x 4/9 = 8/81.
9b. P(G1 and G2) = P(G1) + P(G2) - P(G1 and G2) =
(3/9 + 2/9) - (3/9 x 2/9) = 5/9 - 6/81 = 39/81
9c. P(one R, one Y) = P(R1 and Y2) + P(Y1 and R2) =
(2/9 x 3/9) + P(4/9 x 4/9) = 6/81 + 16/81 = 22/81